Worship in Crisis

by Henry E. Horn

Fortress Press   Philadelphia

Portions of this book originally appeared in an article by the author, "Experimentation and the Congregation," in *Religion in Life,* Vol. XXXIX, No. 1 (Spring, 1970), pp. 8–17. Copyright © 1970 by Abingdon Press. Reprinted with the permission of Abingdon Press.

Library of Congress Catalog Card Number: 79-179631

ISBN 0-8006-1403-8

3166 K71   Printed in U.S.A.   1-1403

Contents

Preface

This book *had* to be written! As chairman of the Commission on Liturgy and the Hymnal of the cooperating Lutheran churches that published the *Service Book and Hymnal* of 1957, I have for long been in the midst of the struggle for new language and new forms for worship. As pastor of University Lutheran Church, Cambridge, I have been besieged with weekly cries for change in worship. Around us, campus ministers have been in the vanguard of experimentation for years. Ecumenical underground congregations are part of our normal life.

It has bothered me to find that very often the persons who know least about the church's tradition in worship are the first to try out new things. No standards of evaluation are ever applied. One goes from one happening to the next with the cycle lasting only a limited time. To this observer, this sometimes appears to be the route of an escapist, an endeavor to bypass the difficult steps in learning an art.

This book will appear conservative to many. That should not be a problem. There are a dozen books on the *new* worship to one on the *tradition*. I just hope that we add some substance to the present debate. The book is addressed very directly to those who have charge of congregational worship in whatever denomination. A good half of the book actually provides a scheme and materials for analyzing one's own worship, developing a program, and providing for renewal.

The first two chapters attempt to survey the present confusion, giving a little background on how we came to our present crisis. Then come several key chapters giving necessary orientation: "Freeing the Imagination," "An Examination of Human Consciousness," "Language and Liturgy." There is much in these chapters which is essential to an understanding of the material that follows. I had intended to have a whole chapter dealing with the theology of worship, but in the interest of brevity and in the method of "doing" theology today I decided to provide comments in depth throughout the whole second part. Much of the material in these chapters has been presented as lectures at the Lutheran School of Theology in Chicago, the Lutheran Theological Southern Seminary at Columbia, South Carolina, and the Lutheridge (North Carolina) School of Church Music. I thank those institutions for the opportunity of testing the material presented in this section.

Starting with "The Christian Tradition of Worship" I am here applying what I suggested in the article "Experimentation and the Congregation" in a symposium on worship in *Religion in Life* (Spring 1970). That chapter outlines the procedure and summarizes the probable direction that an analysis of congregational worship might take. Thereafter, successively, I have dealt with the specific traditions as listed in the introductory chapter of that section.

Frankly, I have not dealt as fully with expression, evangelism, and program as perhaps I should. My emphasis is elsewhere, in areas where I have invested my own talents. I can count on the devotees of those specific aspects to be vociferous in their criticisms and effusive in their additions. That is the way it has to be.

If hints of recent trauma seem to pop out here and there—recognized by those closest to me, the members of University Lutheran Church—at least this full statement of my position is now before their eyes. I will respect their rebuttals if I know they have read the case.

No one can predict where the present currents in worship will take us, but there is no excuse if those at the tiller do not attempt to steer. Right now there is little evidence of any sense of direction. It is my fervent hope that this little book will help Christian communities to involve themselves with a clear sense of direction in the decisions necessary. Everything is to be gained in the renewal of Christian worship.

Part I
INTRODUCTION

"They have removed the landmarks!" This biblical cry is a colorful statement of confusion in a time of change. It was especially descriptive in that land of desert wastes where a cairn of rocks could mean the difference between life and death. The removal of this one landmark could bring forth paralyzing dread.

In their worship, Christian congregations have long placed their trust in well-established forms and orders. Often without learning to know the terrain, they have placed their confidence in what some specialist said was right and proper. Suddenly, within a decade, the accepted standards have now been shaken, and at the same time undisciplined expression has broken out among us. Feeling is in the ascendancy, and understandably so. Protesting against our scientific/technological society, the full emotions which make a man must gain expression.

The results of this upheaval are evident in a general malaise among church people. There are those who rise up to "do their own thing." There are many more who drift away not knowing any longer what to believe. Though worship is central to the church's life, few teachers deal directly with its meaning and with the inherent integrity of each rite. Though experimentation runs rampant, it is rare to find any church agencies that are involved in its evaluation and refinement.

The first two chapters of our present work survey this situation. They set the stage for all that follows. They attempt to do this with broad sweeps of color and shapes, providing the setting within which we must move.

1   Crisis in
Worship

The cover is off! Pandora's box is open! The worship of the church will never be the same! Multimedia shows, jazz masses, rock songs, balloons and placards, "groovy" language, "flicks," and changing lights are here!

Starting in underground, avant-garde, ecumenical communities, a movement of sizeable proportions is with us. Regardless of traditional backgrounds, enthusiasts identify with social change and with the language of ordinary folk. The line between what is done in church and what might be done at a demonstration on a social issue is erased.

The sweep is irresistible. Few congregations can maintain their composure. If one sends youth to conferences or conventions, they come back singing the new tunes and pressing for social change. If one relies on the old ladies to maintain the congregation's sanity, he finds that they too dabble in folk masses at their conventions away from home. The only people who can remain pure are those who never go anywhere and never do anything; but for them to be the defenders of the *status quo* is of small help.

Of course, there are those members—perhaps not a few—who feel deeply with C.S. Lewis:

> I can make do with almost any kind of service whatever, if only it will stay put. But if each form is snatched away just when I am beginning to feel at home in it, then I can never make any progress in the art of worship. . . .
>
> Every service is a structure of acts and words through which we receive a sacrament, or repent, or supplicate, or adore. And it enables us to do these things best—if you like, it "works" best—when through long familiarity, we don't have to think about it. As long as you notice, and have to count the steps, you are not yet dancing but only learning to dance. A good shoe is a shoe you

don't notice. Good reading becomes possible when you need not consciously think about eyes, or light, or print, or spelling. The perfect church service would be one we were almost unaware of: our attention would have been on God.[1]

How much these members just drop out of sight is anyone's guess; certainly the times are not with them. The "movement" will not allow them their peace and quiet. It will rip down the familiar hangings on the east wall and thrust the world's concerns right in their faces.

Here, between these extremes, the congregations must live their lives. We intend to address this problem of the congregation's worship in the midst of change.

Open to Attack

The movement for completely new forms caught the churches off guard. Most of us had been seeking forms and media that had universal appeal and that would bind us to the church-of-all-times. We had just opened ourselves for change in this direction. The discoveries of the late nineteenth and early twentieth centuries had given us a picture of times "when the liturgies were pure." Those were the days when people knew what to do; when the rubrical directions were precise; everything had its time and place; manners were proper; moods were attained with finesse.

But scarcely had we rediscovered these treasures than a new and fresh liturgical wind blew up. And opening our mouths to gulp in this new movement, based upon the actions of worship, we swallowed something else. Innovation of any kind seems to be proper now. One does "his own thing," and all of this is then put together and tied in a knot. Standards for evaluation are limited to popularity; we have swallowed a mouthful of NOW. And in the hangover, we detect some inarticulate problems that have rarely surfaced before.

To oppose the NOW always loads an impossible burden on a person. The NOW is that which is already upon everyone's lips, is clearly stated in words, and is celebrated visually before everyone's eyes. But the *now* that each of us *is*, is something else. It is

4

hidden, unconscious, unexpressed, inarticulate; it always loses to the articulate NOW.

Everyone knows that human life is more than the present wave of consciousness. Few of us act on the basis of that knowledge. There is a whole host of interconnected threads in the deeper part of life that form one's postures, attitudes, bent of life. It is precisely this that we must seek to bring to the surface and express, or we will be forced either to agree or disagree with the *now*. To find out who one is, one has to investigate what one has been.

The fact that we haven't done this is revealed by the pendulum swing in Christian worship through the past decades. Action and reaction: first yes, and then no! It is this changing confusion that baffles the layman. Isn't it possible to communicate one's forms and manners from one generation to the next without the pendulum swing of rejection and reaffirmation? Isn't there some standard of authenticity and integrity for Christian worship that is constant?

Crisis in Authority

The present state of worship is a graphic paradigm of the actual authority crisis within the church in our day. Many of us had been nourished in quiet dependence upon a mystical, traditional authority figure. We trusted this authority because it belonged to the church. There seemed to be nothing wrong with putting all this trust in one particular person who knew what it all was about. The oracle spoke and every church could know where to put its flowers, or where the officiating minister should stand, when he should turn and where. If this was not authoritative for all, the movement toward organizational regularity soon took over a power of its own. Congregations could seek regularity and standardization because they belonged to a national church. In a world of increasing mobility it made sense to provide a single, familiar liturgy in every church.

We haven't fully comprehended the revolutionary changes in church life that took place during the years since the Vatican II Council. Some Roman Catholic writers have demonstrated how influential were the theological and liturgical specialists who advised the bishops at the council and who pushed through their hoped-for changes.[2] These *periti* came to the council well prepared. They were behind all the changes that took place; indeed the bishops probably hardly comprehended what was going on, and ever since have had a hard time interpreting to themselves just what happened. Since Vatican II, furthermore, this theological and liturgical elite has continued to write and to gather a following, unchecked by ecclesiastical authority. They have actually become a new authoritarianism, an avant-garde which is even more authoritarian in its effect on the church simply because it uses the mask of protest against traditional and organizational authority. Some observers now see the emergence of a fourth authority which further clouds church life: the authority of charismatic leaders, persons who through their winsome gifts give promise of bringing others out of the dilemmas of our times. By encouraging their followers to transcend moral limitations, they take creative but very dangerous steps. No one can predict what may happen when they transfer their charismatic authority to other leaders.

Protestants have no trouble seeing in this analysis their own immediate history. For the past several decades, we have had our own *periti* whom we have followed. Theological seminaries have all been dependent upon the Niebuhrs, Dietrich Bonhoeffer, Paul Tillich, J.A.T. Robinson, Thomas Altizer, William Hamilton, etc., and in succession we have bobbed up and down with the times. Today almost any leader with charisma can have his following. Our laity have been beaten down since they have most often been unaware of these great voices, and, when aware, they have refused to be impressed. It is no wonder that the voices for change in worship and church life have been largely those of the clergy, and those who have been in the avant-garde.

Especially effective in its influence has been the bureaucracy of the ecumenical church. Rarely have so few had so much publicity as certain voices in the World Council of Churches, particularly in the former Youth Department. Radical criticisms of traditional church worship starting from this source have, years later, become normal conversation for a whole generation. Which is cause and which is effect will never be known. It is enough to see that what was put forward as a program by several voices years ago has become the assumption of today. Alexander Schmemann, in describing this avant-garde effect upon us, dubs it the "of course" movement. Whenever change is mentioned in worship anywhere, we now say "of course" without ever thinking of any standards of evaluation.[3]

In short, in just a few years the whole supporting environment for the integrity of the church's worship has changed. Whereas a decade ago we always asked what was proper, what does the church do in a particular situation, today we ask how we can change what is before us, how we can do "our own thing"?

But the church is more than the avant-garde or its charismatic leaders. It is the whole body of God's people. Ultimately the authority problem in the church is going to be solved by this whole people. Avant-garde and charismatic leaders must find justification for their authority to the degree that this affects the whole people. The problem of authority is, therefore, much larger than they think. And so is the problem of the church's worship. Only such solutions as involve the whole people in their corporate actions are credible. New liturgies can only be tested by their wearing quality where ordinary folk use them as a vehicle of their regular worship.

Faith in a Secular World

In his book, *Man Becoming*, Gregory Baum has accurately described the plight of a large number of intelligent Christians today:

> A Christian meets his crisis when the spiritual experience of his culture is no longer reconcilable with the religious outlook he has inherited and God seems to be more powerfully present in the former than in the latter. Such a crisis often results in what is called superficially, a loss of faith. The Christian then gives up his religion. But if there are available to him theological methods by which he may reinterpret and reassimilate the inherited religion, he may discover a new unity of religious experience, where the Gospel celebrated in the Church sheds light on and intensifies the Spirit-created redemptive values present in the culture to

7

which he belongs. He may then, as a Christian, transform this culture along the line of its own deepest dimension.[4]

Here, in shorthand, Father Baum has diagnosed accurately the plight of the educated Christian in our day, and has suggested a program.

The "loss of faith" to which he refers is evident throughout our land. Churches which were thriving and filled several years ago are now in the midst of a radical recession. A jittery mood has descended upon American Christianity. Very few congregations have faced the new facts. All of us seem to be caught in the webs of past dreams: of successful stewardship programs, evangelism campaigns, inspirational conferences, financial drives. These fantasies seem regularly to be projected upon our times and more enthusiasm is called for by our leaders.

The passing of years has allowed us to gain a little perspective upon our immediate past. We now see how completely American churches were really caught up in the religious revival of the fifties and sixties, itself a period apart with its own dynamics. That was the period when the natural development of an American theology was set aside for a season in favor of the continental theologies of Barth and Tillich. It was for most Protestants the age of neoorthodoxy. Almost all young men entering the ministry were swept up into a return to the word of God; the liberals were the older men, the biblical enthusiasts were the young. Biblical theology supplied a constant stimulation for biblical preaching. The steady guidance of the Niebuhrs and Tillich steered the movement into the midst of social and political problems, giving it immediate relevance. "Those were the days" when churches burgeoned, preaching seemed on the way back, church renewal was genuine.

The reinforcement which came out of the Roman Catholic reformation—of which Vatican II was only the visible symbol— opened up a brief period of almost ecstatic conversations between fellow Christians of all stripes. The possibility of new conversations and alliances exhausted many of us, but provided marvelous dreams. The consequent collapse of this whole structure so soon after its erection is what has us reeling today.

Historians will find these changes intensely interesting. At this close range it appears that our whole life-style was caught up in a giant bubble of our own making. The sudden bursting forth of the "Third World," the black revolution, the cries of minorities for the necessaries of life, the collapse of colonialism everywhere—broke the bubble. Those of us in the university world received our first shocks at the Strasbourg Conference of the World's Student Christian Federation in 1963. Students took over the conference and turned it sharply toward the world's revolution. Ever since then, every world conference has had its revolutionary youth present, from whatever country, urging the churches to confront the actual world, not just the unreal world where "religious" tasks are performed. They have been insistent upon a man-ward movement as the only honest expression of religion. "God-language" is assumed to be nonsensical.[5]

During these days young theologians also discovered the prison letters of Dietrich Bonhoeffer, especially as he criticized the inept piety of his own day. Bonhoeffer insisted that man has now come of age and must be treated as though he had arrived in strength. Formerly Christianity had ministered to man in his weak places and moments, but in a scientific-technological age this left man without the gospel in exactly those activities in which he wielded power. The "religion" of the past had been a piety apart from man's activities in strength; that "religion" must now be given up for a "religionless" Christianity, that is, a Christianity which eliminates those things which assume man needs God, or that God alone can save him. We must now move into man's world where man is in strength, and there provide new resources for human life. The whole focus of attention is now upon this world, and this secular time.

A few very vocal American theologians, not really aware of the nuances of Bonhoeffer's German or the depth of his ideas, popularized this move toward secular humanism. They denied that "religion" was at all necessary, and urged a radical change in forms of worship, indeed, even the erasure of God-ward activity. The confessions of the Anglican bishop J.A.T. Robinson in *Honest to God* were widely read, and they influenced a large number of the laity. It was not that the negatives about God-talk were that convincing; they were really therapeutic for many who had not grown in their spirituality. Furthermore, the finger pointed to exactly the place where the religious task was to be performed, that is, man's world. One wrote:

> . . . in the time of waiting we have a place to be. It is not before an altar, it is in the world, in the city, with both the needy neighbor and the enemy. This place really defines our faith, for faith and love come together in the interim of waiting. This place, as we shall see, is not only the place for waiting for God, it is also a way to Jesus Christ.[6]

In the midst of this reorientation of many Christians from a God-ward direction of faith towards "man come of age," Harvey Cox's *The Secular City* opened an enthusiastic path for the affirmation of the secular life of the world. Cox provided a bridge by which many could move from their neoorthodox, biblical positions into the new world of man's life. He emphasized the way the Old Testament prophets actually "desacralized" the world. Biblical man was shown to have taken the demons and gods out of nature in order to lay bare the freedom to live in the created world. He found the whole prophetic movement to be against "religion": that activity which attributes divine and mystical presence to things. Having freed things from the powers, he opened up positive possibilities for affirming the secular, created world as the scene of the Christian's life. *The Secular City* is a dated book: it came out at just the right time for the right people. Like a bridge, it served its function, but once the traffic had passed over, one had second thoughts about the structure of the bridge and the bridgeheads. Nevertheless, the bridge worked.

Now, the affirmation that man's world is to be the center of religious activity is firmly established. The World Council of Churches is concentrating upon studies of the new man—the *New Humanum*. Conversations are being opened up with anthropologists, sociologists, and psychologists concerning the problems of man; programmed movements are being devised to aid the "Third World"; preoccupation is intense with racial tensions and the revolutions of minorities.

During the time when Christians were adjusting to this new but extremely obvious movement of their life, it was difficult to see the whole picture. Voices of caution were usually disregarded. They were accused of defending their own turf, and could then be ignored. Particularly ineffective were those who continued to speak in directional terms: of a vertical relationship of man with God, and a horizontal relationship of man with man. The "Bonhoefferian revolution" among American theologians tended precisely towards the elimination of the vertical dimension of life. All is now horizontal: God must be found in human life alone.

One of the great disappointments of the 1968 Uppsala Assembly of the World Council of Churches was the absence of theologians who could effectively come between the old guard who spoke in two-dimensional categories, and the young, so-called secular humanists. Only those Christians who had not been affected by this directional split, particularly the Eastern Orthodox, could cut through this confrontation.[7] They alone recognized that both positions misunderstand the world and God to be two completely separate categories. "Secularization," the consideration of the world apart from God, was to them a quite impossible position for Christians. Their presence in the midst of this battle was a saving grace.

A perhaps more subtle difficulty for the "secular Christian" arises from the very nature of the secular age. To treat man in his strength is to enter into the world of specialization or compartmentalization. Under a religious view of life, however, man is a unity, a whole. Take away the concept of wholeness and everything goes into separate boxes. In each separate category a person develops his own special competence and plays his own role. Life then becomes a number of roles which pull persons in every direction.

Gerardus van der Leeuw has described this graphically:

> The great difficulty, indeed the tragedy of our modern life, lies in the fact that we differentiate between the things that concern us and things which do not concern us. We are musical or we are not: we are religious or we are not. We have our "job" and our "free time"; we drive off on vacations and stare at the natives who work at the resort; and the natives come to us and cannot

imagine what these people are about in all their buildings. We are concerned with politics or we despise all politics as a sordid business. We dance at the ball while wondering at the evolution of the ballet; or we do not dance at all and are annoyed at the crazy acrobatics that claim to be art or entertainment. . . . In a word, we have lost the unity of life. . . .[8]

He goes on to say that primitive man was not necessarily more "religious" than we are. Instead, he held on to the wholeness of life and perhaps then skimmed over the surface of things. We, on the other hand, dig deeply into the heart of things while we lose the breadth of life's meaning.

Today the lonely voice from van der Leeuw in the fifties has become a mighty roar from a whole generation of the young. In an almost pathological way their cry for feeling and wholeness may be a refusal to "come of age." One cannot escape their message. The whole drive toward secularization is misguided. Their anger against science and technology is clear. They have seen what happens when one allows man to compartmentalize his life and then simply bundle these unexamined specialties into a culture.

Eastern religions with their stress on Nature are, for many young persons, the thing. They lead toward wholeness. Similarly, the passion for rock music and the folk idiom is also a recovery of music, movement, dance, touch—feeling for everyone! Feeling implies an opposition to specialized, compartmentalized training and its highly disciplined manners and forms. It implies a warm tolerance for the failures of the beginner and likewise a distaste for those who are locked up tight in their secular compartments.

Maintaining One's Identity

The chief problem for life in a secular world is maintaining one's own identity as a person. Among the many compelling demands for the soul, how shall one maintain wholeness? The claims for loyalty are strident and conflicting. Man is torn apart into different fragments.

But this is not a new problem at all. The pagan in biblical times was typical of secular man today. Sunday was set aside for the worship of the sun, Monday for the moon, and each day thereafter for a specialized relationship. It was impossible for the pagan to be completely involved in the devotion of one day for the next would then demand equal time. He got used to observing the proper ceremonies which would allow him to get through each day, but he could not take everything as seriously as seemed to be demanded. The religious ceremonies therefore automatically took care of his compromises; his life remained fragmented and to find the unity of life a person had either to tranquilize himself with sedation or overstimulate himself into another form of consciousness. This sounds almost exactly like the pathway of modern secular man.[9]

The whole point of the Jewish faith was its concentration upon the Lord who was One and who demanded the wholeness of daily devotion. The great Shema which the Jew was to say several times each day as a fixed devotion was a discipline for fixing the attention of mind and heart on the only all-encompassing truth that brings wholeness to life: "Hear, O Israel, the Lord thy God is One Lord; and thou shalt love the Lord thy God with all thy heart and with all thy strength and with all thy mind." The celebration of the Sabbath, the great day of the week, was so to concentrate upon every moment of this one day as to celebrate the perfection of the created world and thus to transform the whole of time. It was to bring the kingdom of the Lord into the world of man's life —the kingdom of wholeness and peace. The use of short prayers or blessings (*berakoth*) was a discipline whereby the energies of the Creator were thankfully accepted into life, and the created world was opened to that dynamic power. These religious exercises became for the people of God disciplines of a wholeness received from the Lord who is One. That is the heart of Judaism.

Those Christians who have been really sensitive to their biblical heritage will see that the compartmentalization of modern life is actually the challenge for our faith. The urge to wholeness is part of our heritage. Openness to him from whom wholeness comes is part of our identity as Christians. Thus, in a world where everyone seems to run after the latest happening there is a minority whose life is received in faithfulness from the Lord.

In the discussions of the worship of the church which follow, we must remember that the fundamental direction for believers is from God to man. We love because he first loved us. His is the initiatory power. There are those who insist that our age has changed, that no longer will individuals trust themselves to any previous tradition. But for us, "Tradition is the only way we have of knowing who we are."[10]

NOTES

1. See *Letters to Malcolm: Chiefly on Prayer* (New York: Harcourt, Brace, 1964), pp. 3 and 1. Reprinted with permission of the publisher.

2. See James Hitchcock, "Authority in the Church," *Cross Currents* 20, No. 4 (Fall 1970): 376 ff.

3. Alexander Schmemann is remembered from a lecture given at Gettysburg Seminary several years ago. See "Liturgy, Symbol and Sacraments," *Gettysburg Seminary Bulletin* (Winter 1970).

4. See Gregory Baum, *Man Becoming* (New York: Herder and Herder, 1970), pp. vii ff.

5. This was especially noticeable in the reactions of the youth delegation to the Assembly of the World Council of Churches at Uppsala, 1968.

6. Hamilton and Altizer, *Radical Theology and the Death of God* (Indianapolis: Bobbs-Merrill, 1966), p. 41.

7. One thinks particularly of the splendid speeches by Father Paul Vergese to the visitors at the Uppsala Assembly, as well as of the reactions of East European theologians to the praise of the secular coming from the North American and North European theologians. While the latter seemed to predict the end of the congregation, the theologians from oppressed areas put all their confidence in the revival of the parish!

8. One of the seminal books on worship is Gerardus van der Leeuw's *Sacred and Profane Beauty* (New York: Holt, Rinehart, and Winston, 1963), p. 33.

9. See Zalman Schachter, "Patterns of Good and Evil," *Rediscovering Judaism*, ed. Arnold J. Wolf (Chicago: Quadrangle Books, 1966), p. 165.

10. I believe this quotation, long retained in my memory, is from Carl van Doren.

2　A Revolutionary Day

In the midst of the now famous Harvard explosion of the spring of 1969, the president of the university wrote: "Reason and civility, persuasion and respect for differences of opinion—these hard-won conditions for civilized discourse still have their honored place with us. And must have. And will have. . . ."[1] It was clear that the president of the university had in this conflict reached the wall at which he had to take his stand. In his mind, something essential to the university would collapse if this position were not defended.

This statement assumes a whole structure of life providing for "the hard-won conditions for civilized discourse" by which human communities can enter into an educational enterprise. Only upon this platform is there stability for men to develop those arts of learning which require intense concentration, acquired skills, and practiced activity. It belongs to the nature of these processes that one moves from one step of accomplishment to another, and thus a hierarchy of attainment is built-in. Those who then attain the peak can speak of their acquired habits in terms of "good order."

We who observed the "battle of Harvard" from without wondered how it was possible for a university administrator to fail to see the movement of our times. His defense was made in precisely those terms against which the youthful attackers raged: "Reason and civility, persuasion and respect." As several have said about the counterculture, "Their psychedelic experience proclaims the end of scientific, democratic, secular rationalism and a return to the primordial, instinctual, ecstatic irrationalism."[2] The rock idiom "spits at gentility" and cultured manners. Good order itself is the location of the battle. The counterculture is alienated from the whole system of order: its inner authority, its hierarchy of values, its platforms of attainment, its structures of performance, its "good order."

Those of us in university centers have been living in truly apocalyptic times when one can rarely find any common meeting place or method of communication between the culture and the counterculture. It is not that we had no advance warning. Poets, novelists, and artists have been predicting and depicting this rejection of basic assumptions for almost a century. Violence has always had its place within our culture. However, until the twentieth century the accepted manners of Western man have been strong enough to contain this violence within these forms. If there were outbreaks they were episodic; strong restraining forces managed to pull things back into approved forms of expression. Commonly held metaphors continued to be adequate for the imaginations of most people, and to provide room for future movement.

Today we are just beginning to appreciate the tremendous effect of the wars of this century. Since World War I, violence has been loosed upon whole peoples, often completely innocent. The effect of this violence upon literature and the arts was immediate. No longer does art depict the adequacy of restraining forms; violence and four letter words are commonplace. Starting in Europe, this process has now descended upon North America. Forms and manners are the center of attack; they are unable to control the violence.[3]

That is why it was so very troubling to some of us to hear the president of a great university appeal to a return to "reason and civility, persuasion and respect for differences of opinion." These were the forms of that ordered world of the Enlightenment which we left years ago. Precisely these manners have proven themselves unable to control the violence of our times. If a new order is to be found and established, it must be discovered by taking this revolution seriously and discovering with the counterculture new bases upon which to build.

Few descriptions of the generation gap have been as popular as Charles Reich's *The Greening of America*.[4] The author, by oversimplification, describes three different and separate types of

American consciousness. Consciousness I is that of the traditional American farmer, small business man, or worker who has gotten ahead by good hard work and who expects all to follow his example. Consciousness II is the formation of our technical and corporate society which has dealt with things. It finds its joy in manipulating computers and machines and directing the minds and lives of the many toward its own values. Within Consciousness II, Reich manages to classify the whole world of expertise and technical skill which has developed since World War II. Consciousness III, Reich finds, developed in the mid-1960s and now dominates the whole younger generation. Its origins seem to come out of the great promise of life that our cultural and scientific affluence has promised, and also out of the threat to that promise which comes from the pitiful failures of our years: the Vietnam conflict, the shadow of nuclear explosion, ecological disaster, and overpopulation.

Reich's scheme is entirely too simple. Yet it does provide a tool for observing what is happening in our country today. *Something* has happened to turn students violently against our present political leadership as well as against "the system" which grinds on to disaster. Urgent hope and dire disaster are mixed messages from the younger generation as they seek to influence decisions at all levels.

This world is the real one. The church's worship must be set astride the generation gap. We cannot simply accept the position of one generation over against another. We must find the meaning of worship in the very heart of this daily conflict.

If the exposed position of a university president can serve as a target for criticism, what about those of us who have charge of the church's worship? Perhaps there is no other place in our church life where one is so openly exposed to public gaze. Moreover, our worship traditionally follows "good order"; we have our own system of ordering worship, our inner authority, our hierarchy of values, our platforms of attainment, our structures of performance. If trained performers and guilds of workers persist anywhere in the church, we will find them gathered around public worship.

Not only is this true in congregations, we have even developed a hierarchy of specialists in worship and liturgy. Perhaps the process of forming one common liturgy for each denomination led to this. Be that as it may, we have been living for decades under the traditional authority of several voices—of specialists in worship —who know what is right and proper at any time. Their dictatorship has been enforced through the rubrics that tell us what we *shall* do and what we *may* do. We thread our way through these manners with furtive glances at authority to be sure we are doing things properly and in order.

An attack on this whole system has come gradually. Perhaps the first awareness of a change has come to us as the texts of some of our hymns have worn out in the midst of use. They no longer describe the situation of our people, they speak of another, and simpler time. This first happened with missionary hymns. They speak out of nineteenth-century triumphalism and white colonialism, imperialistically and paternalistically emphasizing just those qualities that present racial confrontations find distasteful in us.[5] In the face of a completely changed mission situation, it has been almost impossible to continue to sing these texts with meaning. Pietistic hymns tell a similar story.[6] Private relations with God do not fit a Christianity which has rediscovered its own consciousness as God's people in the world. When we reached for hymns of the kingdom that came out of the liberal movements of the early years of this century, we found them dealing with the world's problems, to be sure, but entirely too heroic and romantic in their expectations.[7] They did not appreciate the tragedies in human life to which the twentieth century has exposed us. By this time, our critical faculties had been stirred in worship, and we found the agricultural setting behind most of the texts rather difficult for translation into the crowded urban megalopolis of our daily experience.

The second point at which we became aware of change was always present. A scheme of forms and manners which requires increasing knowledge and familiarity for positive evaluation, has to have an elaborate educative process. In any art, the novice is quite incapable of judgment; one has to experience various steps of attainment before he can stand back and pronounce judgment. Such delayed evaluation carries with it dangerous potential. There is always the attraction of short-circuiting the process and making premature judgments before one fully comprehends the material. People will not usually wait in patience, assuming that the fathers who established this order were men of wisdom. Indeed, our era of violence has demonstrated that this is exactly what the inexperienced will not do. Instead, they tend to judge their *feelings about the materials* rather than isolate the elements in an issue, then total up both sides and make a judgment. Indeed, some very perceptive thinkers have predicted that we are now in a "post-confessional" period of Judaism and Christianity where no one will start his faith in trust in any institution's tradition.

Some years ago, we saw the signs of the "short-circuiting" phenomenon. Youth departments of the churches deserted their programs of educating young people in the forms the church uses and substituted texts and tunes which came from a semipopular idiom that young people already knew. These paraliturgical items were defended as a sort of bridge by which the young would come to the actual liturgy of the church. The Kyrie was set, for example, to the tune of "Nobody Knows"; the Gloria in Excelsis to "He's Got the Whole Wide World In His Hands." The authors[8] protested that they never intended these materials to take the place of the accepted forms of the liturgy and their intention was honest.

The facts, nevertheless, are that these materials became the bridge, not to the forms which the church uses, but to a freedom for charismatic leaders all through the churches to "do their own thing." Once the guitar was found to be usable in this medium, anyone who could play became a charismatic leader of worship in the "folk idiom." Parallel movements among Roman Catholics in new-found Vatican II freedom gave the movement impetus. After all, those churches which have had little place for the doctrine of the Holy Spirit would be expected to be the ones most open to charismatic influence; they wouldn't know how to control it.

The Youth Department of the World Council of Churches took an unambiguous stand. It advocated a reform of the church's worship along such "folk" lines, its clear assumption being that the forms and manners of the church's own worship had reached a ridiculous stage. In the introduction to *New Hymns for a New Day*, Albert van den Heuvel is clear in his intention when he says:

> There was a minister in a European country not very long ago, who told his congregation on a Sunday morning that they would sing one hymn: "What we should like to sing about," he said, "is not in the hymnal; what is in the hymnal about our subject is obsolete or heretical. So let us be silent and listen to the organ."
> This little story is, of course, irritating. I can already hear lots of people say: but there are beautiful hymns in our hymnal! Our fathers have sung them for many centuries! We have learned them from our mothers! What is wrong with Ambrosius' hymns, Luther's hymns, the Psalms, the Wesleyan treasury, and all the others? The man in our story would have shrugged his shoulders, I am afraid. His point is not that there are no good hymns, but that there are very few that support his preaching and that of his generation. I am with him on this. There are many things in the life of a denomination that are frustrating, but few are so difficult to live with as this one. Choosing the hymns for Sunday morning is an ever-recurring low ebb in my ministry. . . ."

In all of this some of us feel with van den Heuvel. There *are* such times. We do need fresh air . . . and lots of it. But this youth leader pushes ahead:

> This *Risk* is meant to make people unhappy with much that they find in their traditional hymnbooks; it is meant to make people use all their imagination to find new forms. We hope that it means that youth departments of churches will put pressure on their synods and bishops to start using the poets of the land to write new hymns and musicians to write new communal music. . . ."[9]

The type of song urged upon them in *New Hymns for a New Day* does not give hope for an experience of depth which will enrich the worship of the future.

Today we have reached the stage in reform which Alexander Schmemann has dubbed the "of course" stage,[10] when the necessity for reform is so much a fad that everyone merely murmurs "of course." No attempt is then made to analyze needs, clarify standards of renewal, or project ways for evaluating new material. The "of course" is merely the signal for anyone with any idea, perhaps his own speciality, to project it upon a congregation. The mere fact that it is presently in his mind gives excuse for calling it "contemporary" even when the idiom itself is old hat; the fact that everyone is doing it makes the contemporary label doubly compelling. In the absence of any standards for evaluation, the "happenings" are judged by how the attendants feel about them. "Something must have happened because there were so many people who showed up."

One usually appreciates the "happenings" because they are just that: episodic, adrenalin injections into a tired body. If one is forewarned of their occurrence, they can perform a real service in livening a congregation. Perhaps more harmful are the half-hearted efforts of congregations to meet their youth halfway. When one finds adults dabbling as novices in areas where youth are specialists, the results are pretty sorry. How discouraging are those efforts of churchmen who dress up their youth pamphlets with faddish "come-ons" in astrology and the like. The delay that publication causes brings the material on the market when the fad is already passed. The well-thinking writer is then cast in the role of a P.R. man who has come on the scene too late. Nothing seems so hypocritical to youth as this.

The most urgent task facing churchmen today, when they fear that they may have no future, is to guard their integrity, and not to make deals with that which is immediately before them. It is toward that end that this little book has been written.

The Origin of Liturgies

There is a pervading assumption among most of us—possibly because of the present liberty which allows everyone to "do his own thing"—that liturgies are created by gifted writers. It is assumed that a group of people can gather around a table for a number of sessions and then come up with their own liturgy, the resulting creation being fresher and more usable just because it has been recently created. It is further assumed that congregations will accept these fresh creations with grace because they are the creations of flesh and blood contemporaries.

Nothing is farther from the way in which great liturgies have arisen. Indeed, Louis Boyer has shown how these assumptions are precisely those that are prevalent when liturgies are in their death throes.[11] This happens when people play around with that which used to have great meaning.

The opposite is the case. Liturgies have arisen out of the actions of men in dramatizing certain basic assumptions of life's meaning. They are the dramatizations of myths, the imitation of paradigmatic actions. Thus Christian worship centers in such dramatizations: the actions which surround the hearing of a word read from sacred writings and responded to by those who believe this word motivates their lives; or the festal celebration of a sacred meal based upon the Jewish Passover and invested with the meaning of the presence of the kingdom of God in this world. In each case certain essential actions, growing out of the originating form, are basic. Renewal in worship becomes the rediscovery of this essential integrity of each basic action.[12]

How Did We Get Into This Mess?

If we were to compare the most embarrassing incidents in our lives, those times and places where one exhibits the most carefully prepared manners and ways of acting only to find that the rules have been changed without our knowledge would win the prize. Suddenly all serious disciplines and skills are emptied of their honesty and the empty shell accuses us of hypocrisy—"play-acting."

Many of us who have acted as "specialists" in the arts of worship have had such an experience. We were taught that worship was an art. As an art, it could only be learned by careful practice, by the gradual acquisition of skills, by a final grace which was only gained by those who had "the feel." This grace lifted one above the regulations of rubrics and acolyte precisions; it was to provide that easy movement which belongs only to the most gracious connoisseur.

The whole system used to be of one piece, which was a long time coming together. Signs of its approach were present a hundred and fifty years ago when, in the American scene, a native idiom of folk music was forcibly pushed out of our Eastern Seaboard churches by a newly acquired enthusiasm for European scales and musical traditions. We were then taught "what was right." At the same time in England, the Oxford movement "rediscovered" the worship of the medieval church, and the Cambridge movement set Gothic models for church building and furnishings. Authority sounded off in full voice on every side; magazines became oracles for what was proper; the churches made haste to follow. One just left what he was doing and joined the movement. "Of course!"

The recovery of a past tradition became the pattern in that romantic age when the favorite study was history. One imagined what someone else once knew, and it made little difference that the result was somewhat incongruous with reality. After all, churchgoing itself was then actually an escape from present reality and an immersion into an age when the faith was strong and pure.

All of our Christian traditions were examined, and each communion fastened upon some certain time when purity was clear. This became the standard and fixed point from which forms of worship were then redesigned. Once this point had been established, there followed a vigorous period of growth in liturgical knowledge and practice. Manners were then described with some precision; rubrics or directions were made exact; the effects of a past age were reproduced for the present.

This recovery of past liturgical tradition was really a rather marvelous movement in the whole Christian church. Fortunately, a breadth of ecumenicity opened up each tradition to the influence of others. Since everyone was doing it, the process invited cooperation. Certain basic actions of common practice appeared, a common language developed, a common recognition of needs brought leaders of denominational movements together. Denominations managed to bring their variant traditions together, often producing common hymnals and service books, and among the various books of different denominations there appeared many similarities.

The liturgical movement in Roman Catholicism during this past century and a half has been an amazing source of renewal. Long before Vatican II, liturgical reform was already far advanced. Of all the areas discussed by the council, that of liturgical reform was perhaps the best prepared to move—the council merely gave it a shove. The results soon appeared in congregations: services in the vernacular, a return to worship as the *actions* of the people of God, congregational participation. A veritable revolution took place throughout the Catholic world.

It is only surprising that this massive advance of Roman Catholics should not have joined hand in hand with the similar movement in Protestant circles. After all both were moving in parallel directions, particularly in their emphasis on the life of the congregation. Perhaps the Protestants were still a little more involved in their medieval goals at just the time when their own position was rediscovered by the Roman Catholics. At any rate, enriching conversations and mutual development of congregational participation have not occurred.

Instead, something else has happened. The whole focus of our worship has been shifted in the rush to the problems of man. The focal standard of worship in a past age dissolved; the rush came for the NOW, the immediately relevant. And with this change of direction the whole structure of skills and manners came crashing down. When altars are moved away from the walls and become tables, altar guilds with their precise skills evaporate, and acolytes are as confused as dogs in a strange neighborhood; when congregational singing is emphasized, choirs and professional musicians disappear from worship; when the sanctuary is no longer regarded as the symbol of the presence of the living God but becomes the simple meetingplace of the congregation, well-developed habits of orientation collapse, directions of movement are unimportant. Ushers, choirs, guilds, clergy have been left without direction.

And in the confusion it is natural that *feelings* reign. Pushed down so long by a scholastic approach to worship, the way in which people feel had to surface. Some of us can still remember the struggles we had in our early ministry lifting congregations out of their wells of feeling into some objectivity in worship. "He walks with me and He talks with me" was very hard indeed to discourage. Imagine our embarrassment now to have "Amazing

Grace" reappear, championed by the young, while "Put Your Hand in the Hand of the Man from Galilee" lurks dangerously close to the doorway of the church service. All of the stuff we used to sing in our own youth around the camp fires and in youth conferences—stuff that then we would not have dared inject into formal worship—seems to have free access to the church service today. Perhaps we could control all this to a degree were it not for the swelling group of nuns and priests who use their post–Vatican II freedom to compose and create and innovate. There is no defense against this swell of feeling.

For a time we defenders of traditional worship felt that the problem was a simple one of relevance. We knew that we were caught in a romantic reliving of time past. We could easily grant that much of the textual material we used was of agricultural origin, that psalmody presented imagery a little strange to modern man. We tinkered a bit with the language, changing the *Thou*s to *You*s, and smiled in satisfaction only to discover that we had simply provided booby traps for the unsuspecting faithful. Actually, it was the whole enterprise of worship that was being questioned.

Then came the craze to create one's own liturgy, as if the poetic creations of one or two persons can become the authentic medium for the corporate expression of a congregation of people. This turned out to be a most confusing business. One turned naturally to those in the free church tradition, assuming that at least those who had always believed in free prayer could lead us toward a natural expression. But alas, we found there a complete schizophrenia: on the one hand, creative leaders manufactured long, intellectual treatises and called them prayers, or hymns, or acts of worship; on the other, when everyone else was deserting the traditional forms, the free churchmen were beginning to revel in the most hoary of ancient formulas—unfortunately, most often for their aesthetic value. In other words we found they had gone romantic just when we had moved away from this.

If one looked for help from the avant garde, he found an incongruous mess. Perhaps a rock group was invited in to "do its own thing" and numbers were interspersed in the midst of the traditional liturgy. No clear thought would be given to what was happening. The sign of modernity seemed to be present in the form of what is popular.

Well, this is where we are presently. There are some current writers who rejoice that at last the door has been opened, the worship of the church is now ready for the discoveries of intuitive man. Thus John Killinger writes *Leave It to the Spirit* offering material "on the way to becoming *many* books."[13] His successive chapter headings form separate wells from which the innovative may draw freely: forms, games, dance, body, persons, drama, story, language, blasphemy, sermon, music, time/space, meta-worship. One can imagine the variety and richness of these sources. It is certainly an exciting development today that brings all of these resources into the service of the worship of the church.

Our concern in this volume, however, is first and foremost with the integrity of the Christian rite. To consider the tradition from this angle is not to be at all negative to the wonderful resources at hand. Indeed, once we know what we are doing we can bring in enough new forms to transform worship. But the integrity of our rite is the given which must not be changed. Our faith is our response to this given reality.

NOTES

1. Quoted from the report of President Nathan Pusey for 1969.

2. See Andrew Greeley in *Religion in the Year 2000* (New York: Sheed and Ward, 1969), p. 55, and Benjamin De Mott, *Supergrow* (New York: E. P. Dutton Co., 1969), pp. 53 ff.

3. See Frederick J. Hoffman, *The Mortal No: Death and the Modern Imagination* (Princeton, N.J.: Princeton University Press, 1964).

4. See Charles Reich, *The Greening of America* (New York: Random House, 1970).

5. Examples:

> "Can we whose souls are lighted
> With wisdom from on high,
> Can we to men benighted
> The lamp of light deny?"

"Give of thy sons to bear the message glorious,
Give of thy wealth to speed them on their way,
Pour out thy soul for them in prayer victorious,
And haste the coming of the glorious day."

6. Examples:

"I need Thee precious Jesus,
I need a friend like Thee,
A friend to soothe and pity,
A friend to care for me."

"I heard the voice of Jesus say,
'Come unto me and rest,
Lay down thy weary head, lay down
Thy head upon my breast. . . .' "

7. Examples:

"Rise up, O men of God!
The church for thee doth wait!
Her strength unequal to her task,
Rise up and make her great!"

8. I refer to Ewald Bash and John Ylvisaker's *Songs for Today* (Minneapolis, Minn.: American Lutheran Church, 1963). This was a splendid effort for its time. My criticism is aimed at the use that many are making of this opportunity to bypass the liturgy of the church.

9. See Albert van den Heuvel in *Risk*, vol. 2, No. 3 (1966). Also published in *New Hymns for a New Day* (Youth Department of the World Council of Churches and the World Council of Christian Education, Geneva, Switzerland), pp. 5 and 7. Reprinted with permission of the publisher.

10. See above, p. 14, n. 3.

11. See Louis Bouyer, *Rite and Man: Natural Sacredness and Christian Liturgy* (Notre Dame, Ind.: Notre Dame University Press, 1967). This is, in my opinion, Bouyer's best book and a splendid correction for those of us who have been brought up in the Protestant tradition.

12. Of course the language, the visual surroundings, the accompanying music, the actions of the people, must move with the times. There is abundant room for new materials. Perhaps our past dream of one ultimate "service book and hymnal" with all the resources neces-

sary for worship was too grandiose. After all, one ought to place only tested materials in such permanent form, and the tests of usage require several decades. Add to this the time of preparation and such a book cannot but be twenty-five years out of date at its appearance! In our changing world we cannot afford to be that far out of date in our expressions of worship. Loose-leaf editions and inserts will be with us from here on out.

13. See John Killinger, *Leave It to the Spirit* (New York: Harper & Row, 1971), p. ix.

Part II
REORIENTATION

One would expect that a book on worship would start out with a definition of Christian worship. Instead, Part II attempts to re-orient the reader toward aspects of his ordinary life which are essential to corporate worship as a human activity.

When the Samaritan woman met Jesus at the well, she wanted to converse about the God she imagined. Jesus brought her right back to human life by replying: "You worship what you do not know; we worship what we know, for salvation is from the Jews" (John 4:22). In a similar manner we wish not first to consider the meaning of the words *worship* and *God*, but rather to explore the breadth and depth of our human life, and the tools given us to explore it.

We have isolated three fundamental problems in thinking about corporate worship. First, to perform an act of worship is to *imagine* a value or power within or above the ordinary. To worship is in some way to imagine. To use a language of worship is to exercise the imagination. The problem of language in worship today is largely a problem of a stunted imagination. Therefore we must attempt to free the imagination before we can approach renewal.

Second, though man is fundamentally a *social* animal, several centuries of the development of private life and individual consciousness have all but submerged our consciousness of our social reality. Nothing is so unpopular today as one's institutional self; we retreat madly from affirming our social role. Yet public worship is an expression of a social group, and it must use an "objective" language. To face the renewal of worship today, one must find an honest way to express his feelings in a corporate expression. This is perhaps our biggest hurdle.

Third, the act of corporate worship uses *language* in a particular way. This requires an oral style which can be remembered, reused, and which grows in the process. In the rush for new expression, problems of style have been almost totally ignored. The setting of an oral style in the midst of meaningful movements, actions, and feelings is a challenge which enlarges the task of renewal.

We could have extended this reorientation to include many of the radical changes in the mood and setting of Christian worship that have come out of the recent renewal in the churches. We feel, however, that these are covered in other books on worship appearing today.

Part II contains the substantive part of our argument, the reasons why the tradition of the church still demands attention. It also shows up the shortcomings of many of our current attempts at renewal. Here is where we are right now. But our interest is not to be limited to the traditional. Where with new material we follow the principles which Part II lays down, new and adequate pathways will be formed for the future.

3 Freeing the
Imagination

Children are born with the most astonishing gifts. During the early years of childhood, parents are the chief witnesses of an outpouring of creativity which expresses itself in a natural feel for shapes, colors, symbols, and often even for perspective. Robert Motherwell, the artist, suggests that one great miracle of hope for man is the existence of a native art in children the world over. Therein is contained, prior to previous communication, a single language centering around about a dozen symbols.[1]

I have a son who was most gifted in the visual arts as a child. He held his pencil in the most unorthodox but creative way. With it he shaped his conceptions of the world in large, beautiful forms and colors, always doing this in a most playful manner. Once he went to organized school, however, all that ceased. The first visible change came when his teacher told him that we do not hold our pencils that way but *this* way. His poor hand is still cramped because of its resistance to the imposed change. A second stage of adjustment could be seen in the pictures he still drew on corners of papers—after he had completed the assignments for which he received the applause of the adult world. These microscopic creations still showed some of the shapes and perspectives of his native gift, but they actually depicted apocalyptical scenes of violence, expressions of his evident anger over the imposition of an adult culture upon his own imaginative creations. The third stage was the submergence of the gift itself.

The Shape of Intuition

His story is the story of a whole generation. No wonder that the counterculture should focus its attention at exactly those places where one's native gifts come into conflict with the accepted standards of the adult world. They have experienced that anger again and again. It is not surprising that the most popular vocation among them is to take the place of those teachers who presided over the meetingplace between the child's native gifts and the prevailing culture. Their excitement about expressive and creative methods of primary and elementary education is well placed.

Heretofore not much attention had been given to the shape of the native gifts of childhood. Most of the time we regarded those gifts as primitive, shapeless impressions lacking in inner logic. The fact that all children everywhere have such a universal language was either missed, or its own logic was ignored. Recent studies, however, have begun to reveal a form to all of this. In a remarkable study, Anton Ehrenzweig attacks this problem, proposing that a child's visual art projects the shapes, images, and metaphors which become the vessels to carry his thinking.[2] One can see in these forms the conceptual framework that holds the child's world together. In other words, these shapes are not merely the inchoate outlines of the child's subconscious, as had been previously thought, but rather they are that assumed, unconscious world of postures, forms, shapes which the child formulated before self-consciousness took over his life. Thus they are ready vessels for carrying the material of conscious thought.

With this assumption, Ehrenzweig finds the danger point right where this assumed, unconscious world comes into collision with the accepted standards of the adult world. One has to be extremely careful of his values at this point. If adult standards are affirmed too strongly over against the child's inarticulate assumptions, the world of the child withers; on the other hand, without some positive evaluation of what is accepted as traditional culture there would be no incentive for the child to enter into that culture, no incentive to learn. The sensitive problem is to knit the two worlds together in positive effort, to join expression with empathy.

In this dilemma between two cultures, one could argue for either side, depending upon just what values should be preserved. We see this argument all around us now: between the traditional and the creative, and between the accepted norms and individual expression. But this conflict merely illustrates where the battle is joined, it does not help toward a resolution. Ehrenzweig goes on to point out what is lost when the child's own world is destroyed. With it goes the whole world of play, as something quite distinct and separate from the work-a-day world. For he finds the large sweeps of color and shapes to be that playful part of art which lifts it above precise and technical work. This is the part which puts everything in proper perspective—the way the piece looks when one steps back from detail and is overwhelmed by the conceptual shape and color of the whole. It is the part of a piece of music which carries one along and allows the mind actually to wander through suggestive pathways until the urgent, precise chords call us back to attention again. There is, then, a direct line of continuity between the child's expression in such forms and colors and the adult's later ability to find the rhythm of play and work which is the source of imaginative creativity. In short, what is at stake in children's art is the ability to play in later life.

The suggestive discoveries of Ehrenzweig remind one of the work of psychologists in the field of cognitive learning. Thus Jerome Bruner in *On Knowing: Essays for the Left Hand*[3] uses the figure of the left hand to represent the intuitive powers of man's mind—precisely those that deal with shapes and colors and forms; the right hand stands for precise, analytical powers used in purposeful, logical, planned endeavor. Bruner maintains that the great creative jumps in man's knowledge come somehow when the left hand intersects with the efforts of the right; new shapes are brought forth to contain the material one is working with; all then suddenly fits into the new forms in a promising way. He calls this moment, the moment of "creative surprise." He then attempts to develop guidelines toward a discipline that can create the conditions for such moments.

Psychological Shapes

From psychological studies come the same general conception of a person's psychological and ethical progress. Models and forms probably precede ideas; one's reactions to life's experience are always poured into the available vessels. Within this system one gains his own confidence in the adequacy of these various vessels. But in an ever widening, pluralistic, relativistic world, a man's models are challenged again and again. Each challenge brings forth anxiety and resistance. No one really wishes to change. But if there is proper stimulation, one overcomes his anxiety by adapting and adjusting his models, changing them slightly to fit the new information he has received.

Persons at work in the college and university would have had a wonderful time lately exposing themselves to a new scheme of the development of college students.[4] From an extremely careful study of selected students over a decade, nine specific steps have been established through which students move from a very protected, limited, authoritarian, and closed world into the midst of our modern relativistic, pluralistic situation, and in this mess find both something to build their lives around and a style of professional performance. Every step is fraught with possible failure; not all students make the journey. Many temporize, some try to escape, some retrogress and harden in a past model of life. Those who grow do this by successive stages that can be studied and exposed to view. At every step of the way dynamics of anxiety and resistance encounter those which pull toward growth. Some of us are excited about the study because it reveals that hidden and dynamic area of life's growth where we are immersed in work. The shape discovered is confirmed by our experience.

The Imagination

Now in this whole process it is obvious that the key dynamic for forward and future movement is what we call the imagination. To imagine is to think in shapes. To be imaginative is to be able to move around many shapes and forms within which experience can find new development. Of course, any experience we have is always seen in the past. We can only see it, talk about it, articulate it as a past event. Therefore the act of remembering is an essential part of bringing an experience into the present, of representing the experience in recognizable form. And this representation is always done in shapes which the imagination forms around the events and persons of our experience. The very act of memory has to be intended, and this intention is stimulated by a desire to remember.

We have had to sketch some of these dynamics to show how the imagination is essentially connected with the past. One shouldn't wonder that so often the shapes and forms within which the imagination carries the past to the present are "out of date." There is a sense in which this just has to be.

On the other hand, there is a necessary future thrust of the imagination. One must be able to project shapes and forms which are adequate to hold his very latest experience. Because it is so painful constantly to change one's metaphors, or vessels of meaning, when one is changing them he wants to be sure that the new ones will be able to contain every conceivable new experience. There must be a potency and enthusiasm for these new forms as possible vehicles of a wider experience. In his introduction to his *The Search for a Usable Future,* Martin Marty has summed this all up: "Men act, in large measure, in the light of the futures which they envision or project. But the raw material for their action comes from remembered ideas, words, events, images, and models. Thus their search for usable futures in any era will be grounded in their view of particular pasts."[5] If imagination is the name we give to the whole dynamic process by which one reaches into the past for forms and projects usable ones on the future with hope, and if precisely this power is presently being ruthlessly destroyed in the education of the new generation, we get some glimpse of the problem before us—to free the imagination.

The Plight of the Imagination

Now thus far our description of the plight of the imagination has been a general one. One could write volumes describing the causes for this. Certainly the overwhelming emphasis on science and technology in the past centuries has overdeveloped the analytical powers of man's mind at the expense of the intuitive powers. Urban life and its encouragement of anonymity has evaporated conversations between crowded peoples; mass media have silenced porch conversations in favor of dumb, auditory receptions of canned addresses. In every conceivable way the imagination of man has been discouraged from its own work.

But how shall we approach the plight of the imagination in the church's worship? Here our present problem is specific. The forms for our imagination in worship have been intensely developed over the past century with a precision rarely equalled in Christian history. The source of these forms can now be located in the Oxford and Cambridge revivals in the early nineteenth century. Normative standards for liturgy and ceremonial were placed in the late medieval period; standards for church architecture were located in the Gothic style. Authorities were developed, official standards were promulgated, evaluation was carried on on the basis of these standards. To imagine in the church's worship was to remember what used to be; the imagination was centered upon what someone else once knew. The memory part of the imagination was overtaxed. The authority on worship was always the antiquarian, the professor of liturgics who answered all questions of propriety, who wrote the rubrics for ceremonial.

When the imagination is overburdened by the memory of what someone else once knew, it becomes useless for the task of enlarging the present forms to make way for new life experiences. One can only do this when the imagination is fastened upon what *he* knows and what *he* experiences. Only a very romantic reconstruction of the past—which never existed—can perpetuate such a misplaced imaginative effort; but there is then no way at all for dealing with the present and the future. Without forms for imagining the life of faith in the present and future, there is no hope of the Christian actually expressing his faith in his daily life. No wonder our children have labeled the traditional "church piety" they saw as phony; no wonder they react negatively against any space being set aside for "religious rites."

The results of this romantic concentration upon past norms are evident in our church life today. On the one hand, we are now increasingly conscious of the inadequacy of our traditional worship to deal with our daily life. We have concentrated upon past forms for several centuries during the rise of the era of science, technology, the city, mass transportation, mass communication, racial and ethnic strife, etc. Rarely is there any reference to this real world in our traditional hymns and liturgies. Of course, the demand for relevancy is long overdue, despite its excesses.

On the other hand, there are a host of very fine church people who have taken traditional standards with great seriousness, who have entered into traditional skills and have mastered them, and who are now completely confused. The tradition actually nourishes them, informs their imaginations, and inspires them to see the whole world in Gothic figures—certainly a legitimate way of life. After all, there is much more to this than meets the eye. A whole system of skills nourished the system; a host of acolyte minds still keeps up its esprit de corps; a large number of well-intentioned lay people are still imprisoned in its rubrics.

We cannot just leave this problem with the two sides shouting at each other. That is actually what is happening. Congregations provide the traditional liturgy *or* experimental liturgies and each shows little influence on the other. The first is carefully controlled according to the accepted directions without the least bit of new life that would make it attractive; the latter are often mere cries of protest, often using appropriate forms of shock treatment— howls of anger which simply confuse simple people.

Lost to the church is that lively imagination which fashions the whole context within which any worship can happen—the imagination which hangs new pictures around the walls of the mind, which opens up the nostrils for odors of gratitude, which stimulates the feet to dance. Fortunately now, all of this is coming back to us. The donors of these new gifts are those who were the recipients of our largesse years ago.

Imagination Comes Alive

Hans-Ruedi Weber gave us an indication of what was in store for all of us, years ago, when he wrote about his first experiences as a missionary among the illiterates of Indonesia:

> The more intimately the Western theologian came to know them, the more he was amazed at their powerful imagination, their abil-

ity to see: pictures, actions and significant happenings in nature and human life. Many of these illiterates revealed themselves as true artists in observation and communication. . . . The Western missionary who had come to teach became the pupil. The longer he who had come as a literate among illiterates lived with these "letter-blind" people, the more he realized that he himself was blind among those who could see; that he was a stunted poor intellectual with only *one* means of communication (through pallid, abstract ideas) among imaginative artists who thought and spoke in colourful, flowing pictures and symbols.

If we were to pass on to illiterates the message of the Bible, we must first liberate this message from the abstract ideas of our catechisms and doctrines. We must learn, and use, the illiterate's method of communication. We must proclaim picturesquely and dramatically rather than intellectually and verbally.[6]

Today many of us who have not traveled overseas have gone through a confrontation experience with our black neighbors, and have been opened into this conversion experience. As long as we continue to think in terms of our white affluent superiority, our approach to others is always clouded by paternalism. We reinforce our superiority even in the act of giving. There is just no way in which we are open to the gifts which the recipient of our generosity has to offer. But in confrontation, the tables are turned. They are the givers and we the recipients. And suddenly we realize how "uptight" and narrow-minded we are. Our "tradition" is seen to be a constricting remembrance of things past, many of them deprived of their juice and joy by the confining walls of an impoverished memory. The result of such a conversion experience is an open door for the imagination.

Fortunately, anthropological, psychological, and sociological studies of man are today expanding our knowledge of ourselves. It is hard to keep up with everything, although our own young seem to absorb it all. I remember that in the early sixties Eric Routley wrote an excellent book, *The English Carol*,[7] in which he traced the origin of the carol to those situations in life when man faces an impossible task and all he can do is to cry out. The rhythm of such cries can raise the anchor of a ship, lay iron rails for the railroad, do the work of machines. Routley bewailed the death of the carol because of the appearance of the mechanized and electronic world. No impossible tasks—no songs! Well, the sixties overcame that situation. They provided human tragedies in terrifying progression, and out came the folksongs, genuine ones which gripped a generation. How can we fail to see in this the expression of a released imagination?

This return to intuitive, symbolic expression has caught the churches in midstream. Since the midfifties we had come to our senses, had seen the necessity of modernizing our liturgy. Our emphasis shifted to highlighting the actions of worship. It was assumed that by removing the trappings and opening up the essential actions comprehension would be attained.

Two problems remain, however. When we get all of our actions cleaned up and tidy, we find that the whole action of worship is questioned by modern man. When we move in the direction of rationality, and remove the imaginative context of worship, the whole enterprise loses its significance. The Eucharist demands a vigorous act of the imagination. One cannot simply invest an ordinary meal with special significance. Every action in the Eucharist is surrounded by symbolic meaning.

Unfortunately, church people have started to move in the direction of reason and relevancy just when our own young people have moved in the opposite direction. A Roman Catholic sociologist has described this process wittily:

> It fascinates me in many ways: the hippies and the Merry Pranksters are putting on vestments and we're taking them off; we have stopped saying the rosary and they're wearing beads; we are putting aside our Roman collars and they're donning turtle-necks and Nehru jackets; we are urging our bishops to have no part of pectoral crosses and they are wearing neck jewelry; we are making our new low-church liturgy as symbol-free as possible and they are creating their own liturgy which is filled with romantic poetry and symbolism. This is another manifestation of what I once called Greeley's Law. Greeley's Law goes as follows: As soon as everybody else starts it, Catholics stop it.[8]

Of course, there is now in the churches a movement to correct this. The avant-garde is producing great celebrative events with rock music, multimedia communication, psychedelic atmosphere, strobe lights—the works. Every attempt is being made to surround the ordinary with the extraordinary. The extraordinary always appears from the profane side of life and is mixed with the usual worship to provide a shock treatment.

The Backdrop of Worship

The sociologist Robert Bellah was once asked to be a witness at such a multimedia mass. His solemn criticism is a healthy one:

> There must be, of course, links between the worship service and the immediate, personal and social reality of the worshipers. But even when attained, the element of "relevance," so highly regarded today, is only the first shaky step. Unless there is a link between the religious symbols making up the worship ceremony and the particular past and present of the worshipers, then the worship process cannot begin. Indeed, the more deeply the symbols do grasp the real problems and conflicts of the worshipers, the more powerful the subsequent experience can be. But what happens in worship is the transformation of the personal into the transpersonal, the immediate into the transtemporal. Through this transformation the immediate problems and conflicts can be seen in a new light, insight can be achieved and post-worship changes in behavior can ensue. How we evaluate these changes, which may range from fleeing to the desert to starting a social revolution, depends on our values and is not at issue here. But the point is that the mythical, archetypal, timeless character of religious symbols provides a perspective relative to everyday reality without which, in Blake's words, the latter would "stand still unable to do other than repeat the same dull round over again."[9]

I am sure that many wise heads in our congregations are nodding vigorously at this comment.

Of course, the imaginative backdrop of Christian worship is highly confusing. Layer after layer of various backdrops have been set up for specific times and, like many things in the church, no one ever seems to put any of them away. The whole confusing mass, layer after layer, is presented to us in psalms, Scriptures, hymns, architecture, symbols. We are oversymbolized with ancient Christian mottos and cryptograms. They cry out from every pew end. A host of children have escaped the encounter with the genuine Christian faith in life, because of time spent by their teachers uncoding Christian symbolism which wasn't worth the effort. There is a mass of ossified tradition which must be broken up with a percussion drill if the memory is to fasten vividly upon forms and images that are potent enough to contain our hope for the future.

This problem has been dramatized by Jean Daniélou in his *Theology of Jewish Christianity*.[10] Here he describes one specific backdrop which has formed the background of Christian worship, that of Jewish Christianity. This particular cosmic context for the Christian story was imagined by apocalyptical writers of the inter-testamental period, and the post–New Testament period. It contains such metaphors and figures as that of heaven, of God as King, of his heavenly court, of the hierarchy of various powers and dominations of the spiritual realm, good and evil as opposing forces, angels, the ruling Lord, the Lamb that was slain, etc.—all pictured in writings such as Ezekiel, Daniel, Revelation, and a number of other writings. They are all familiar to our hymnody. In his study he suggests that this is just one possible context for the Christian story—surely not a necessary one—and that possibly this whole backdrop *could* be pulled up. But he warns us that in our day where we are caught in the battle between personal and impersonal forces, between freedom and fate, it might be well to keep exactly this backdrop until we get another that will fill its function:

> If therefore we would in this age bring to troubled mankind the salvation which only Christ can give, we would do no worse than ponder the vision of Jewish Christianity, for which saving faith meant the knowledge that there was indeed wisdom in things, the certainty of the fulfillment of God's Grand Design ordained from the foundation of the world; for which Christ was Lord not only of the heart but of the heavens; for which Baptism was a partaking in the cosmic conquest of evil; and for which the ultimate hope was to follow the Son into the heavenly places and to hear the Thrones and Dominations cry, "Lift up your heads, O ye gates: the King of Glory shall come in."[11]

That is quite a peroration. Perhaps the point can be made more modestly in a homely illustration. Some years ago, an enterprising group of very talented young people in our university parish, enflamed with the very obvious worldly thrust of the liturgical movement, transformed our traditional Anglican chancel space. They removed the huge dossal on the east wall which reminded worshipers of a holy space, a tabernacled presence. They then opened up the space where formerly there were choir pews. Then they provided a eucharistic celebration which was obviously that of the present people of God gathered around the table. Social needs were obvious through the banners. The chancel was no longer to be a holy place within which one should come to pray and meet the presence, it was simply the meeting place of the eucharistic community. If there was no Christian community using the space, it could be used for other purposes. The east wall became a display wall for artistic creations, or a projection wall upon which one could throw a multimedia presentation.

The pastoral problem for me assumed huge proportions. One generation was obviously shouting No to another. Meanwhile the Christian memory, of necessity caught in the past, was hung up in remembered symbols despite all of the drama in trying to reorient it. I have always felt that the transformation might have been more successful if the imagination had been focused not upon the relevant present, but upon the future. It is not by accident that early church tradition always reserved the space behind the table for some representation of the Christ who comes to us and saves us. Their urgent cry, "Maranatha, come, Lord Jesus!" suggested this. From the East comes our salvation.

How I wish now to have some creative artist imagine this coming of our salvation in terms of a cosmic Christ who moves to us through the symbolic representation of our own world of science and technology, of poverty and distress, through pollution and overpopulation! Such an imaginative picture of the future would be the transcendent meeting ground for all pieties. And we would not be in danger of losing that gift which is the most excellent of all—*love.*

43

REORIENTATION

NOTES

1. See Robert Motherwell, "The Universal Language of Children's Art, and Modernism," *The American Scholar* (Winter 1970/71).

2. See Anton Ehrenzweig, *The Hidden Order of Art* (Berkeley: University of California Press, 1967).

3. See Jerome Bruner, *On Knowing: Essays for the Left Hand* (Cambridge: Harvard University Press, 1962).

4. See William G. Perry, Jr., *The Intellectual and Ethical Development of the College Student: A Scheme* (New York: Holt, Rinehart, and Winston, 1970).

5. Martin E. Marty, *The Search for a Usable Future* (New York: Harper & Row, 1969), p. 11.

6. See Hans-Ruedi Weber, *Communicating the Gospel to Illiterates* (New York: Friendship Press, 1957), pp. 18 ff.

7. See Eric Routley, *The English Carol* (New York: Oxford University Press, 1959).

8. See Andrew Greeley, *Theology in Transition,* ed. George Devine (Staten Island, N.Y.: Society of St. Paul, 1970), p. 26.

9. Reprinted with permission. From *Multi-Media Worship:* A Model and Nine Viewpoints by Myron B. Bloy, Jr. Copyright © 1969 by The Church Society for College Work. Published by The Seabury Press, Incorporated, New York, p. 54.

10. See Jean Daniélou, *Theology of Jewish Christianity* (New York: Henry Regnery Co., 1964).

11. Ibid., p. 405.

4   An Examination of
Human Consciousness

Some of us who are most closely associated with the counter-culture have been deeply moved by the revolutionary drive of the young. Many highly idealistic young people throw themselves into the movement for a better America, find themselves deeply tied to minority groups in protest, then join in vigorous acts for reform which fail. From this they move to the other end of the spectrum, toward total rejection of the structures and the system of life, and they seek some unity of feeling through Eastern religions, meanwhile attempting some form of communal living.

In this process a whole element of life drops out of their experience. For with the discarded structures goes a whole way of life through which one controls just how much of himself he will expose through public roles he plays. Without any public self, the individual is totally exposed. He has to respond with some personal integrity to every single stimulation with his whole self. And we are just not adequate for that!

As a result, these young people protect themselves by cutting down the number of contacts they make. They gather in small communes where such limited responses are possible, often seeking loneliness and social suicide. Isolated places often find colonies of such persons, seeking like lemmings to get as far away as possible from what they consider to be a corrupt and rotten society. The whole picture is one of mass suicide.

Man—A Social Animal

For whether we like it or not, man is a social animal. His whole being is a social one. His ability to move within his milieu depends upon a well-developed social consciousness as well as his own private consciousness. We need not belabor the point. Any studies of man's learning processes demonstrate the social character of every learning act, our dependence upon others for models of thought, our sharing of common images which stimulate the imagination. Culture is a commonly shared world of these acts, images, and pictures.

While everyone accepts this as a fact, we have not dealt sufficiently with the implications of the fact. We tend to imagine the cultural world, the structures and systems of life, as some objective things out there! Of course there is justification for this in our scientific and technological world. We have succeeded in pretty well omitting the personal element in such a culture; and the structures do appear to be things out there. It is then easy to assume that it is our own private life which contains the personal element which stands over against the structures.

Lost in these changes is the whole fabric of social consciousness: the skills to act within the social context, to play a role, to understand other persons in their roles, to control what and how much of the self will be revealed in corporate actions. This fabric is regarded as dishonest by the new generation. Instead, movement toward the social context is held to be honest only if it moves within the private sphere and gradually adds to knowledge through a personal revelation of the self. The "T-group" self-revelations, and the opening up of feelings tell the truth about social gatherings, revealing what is happening below the surface.

The Language of Social Consciousness

It is no wonder at all that public corporate worship should suffer from such a change. The whole structure of liturgical acts is corporate; it belongs to the social consciousness, not to the private consciousness. Yet in latter years with the move toward judging everything from the private consciousness, the whole meaning of corporate worship has been warped. Naturally criticism has centered on the forms used.

Years ago, Abraham Heschel saw this happening in American religious life.[1] He maintained that the life of prayer and worship is really dependent upon two opposing poles, expression and empathy. First, the pole of expression defends the private sphere of the religious life, one's own feelings. One must express what is in one's heart and cry out to Reality. But there is the other pole, empathy. One also enters into a religious community which is already there, with its language, images, and symbols. At the pole of empathy, one feels his way into words and symbols already pregnant with meaning.

In determining which is more important, Heschel insists that what is needed is the expression of one's own inner feelings. But perhaps the way for this to happen is a little more complicated than would seem to be the case. For to express one's inner feelings in words is exactly what we today cannot do! The very scientific, technological culture that stands over against us has withered our abilities to converse, to open to one another as persons, to articulate our life. The way back to expression, to Heschel, is through empathy, that is, through feeling oneself into the words of others:

> Those who plead for the primacy of expression over the prayer of empathy ought to remember that the ability to express what is hidden in the heart is a rare gift, and cannot be counted on by all men. What, as a rule, makes it possible for us to pray is our ability to affiliate our own minds with the pattern of fixed texts, to unlock our hearts to the words, and to surrender to their meanings. The words stand before us as living entities full of spiritual power, of a power which often surpasses the grasp of our minds. The words are often the givers, and we are the recipients. They inspire our minds and awaken our hearts. . . . Every one of us bears a vast accumulation of unuttered sorrows, scruples, hopes, and yearnings, frozen in the muteness of our natures. In prayer, the ice breaks, our feelings begin to move our mind, striving for an outlet. Empathy generates expression.[2]

Heschel has pointed to a very obvious fact of our experience as social beings. There is a vast difference between these two poles, expression and empathy, and in the shape of actions that each generates.

Let me illustrate by a homely example. In a large family, one often has several types of children. There is the eighteen-month-old child who is the perfect model of expression. He has a shrill scream for orange juice at breakfast, a grunt for toast. His mother knows what each communication means, and for her own peace of mind attempts to answer the language before it becomes too strident. These expressions are quite inarticulate in a crowd of eighteen-month-old infants, but the loving mother recognizes them as the cries of the stomach, and satisfies them. Just so does the Spirit and the Father work with the children of God. There is no argument over the integrity of this expression. It comes directly from the gut. That kind of honesty is in high favor today. Unfortunately, it is perhaps the only type of honesty which is generally recognized.

There are children at other ages too. Here, for instance, is the high school crowd. They talk together at the dinner table, monopolizing the conversation. Jumping into their speech are words and images from the counterculture, or from their own school classes. These are usually recently acquired, so recently that it is obvious they are slightly embarrassed in the use of these terms. But the demands of NOW, their need to *belong* push them into their use. The parents hear the terms and wink at each other. They would be quite insensitive if they stopped the conversation with, "Hey, what's with that word! Do you really mean that?" After all, the whole process of going to school is that of entering into new communities of human learning, each with its own language, images, symbols, and roles. There is a whole world of development awaiting the neophyte within each of these communities. The first stages are extremely embarrassing as one "puts on" the new language like a uniform, and seeks to live within it. We wouldn't think of stopping a neophyte at this point and accusing him of hypocrisy, or not really meaning what he said, of not feeling the part he is playing. Of course the neophyte lives in a double world; of course, he is playacting and therefore hypocritical in the root meaning of that word. But the quality of one's honesty in this social situation is quite different from that of simple private expression.

Now, as one stands back and surveys these two poles, expression and empathy, it becomes clear that the cultural development of man is actually centered in the pole of empathy. That is the way we grow. We know this so well, too well in our scientific, technological culture. For the very symbol of this culture is the lab coat and the quiet technical conversation. Perhaps it is this symbol that the counterculture rejects in its race for privatism and feeling. Certainly Professor Reich in *The Greening of America* has set these two forms of consciousness over against each other without suggesting any hope for the future.

A New Look

There are some, however, who are urgently calling for a new look at these two forms of consciousness as essential partners in every man's approach to himself. Thus Peter Berger and Thomas Luckmann, in their excellent little book, *The Social Construction of Reality,* have centered upon the missing dimension of our thinking of ourselves as social beings.[3] Since man is by nature a social being, he is formed by conversations, articulate and inarticulate, with others and with his environment. Berger and Luckmann describe two levels of socialization. The first, primary socialization, refers to that which makes a human being human: that conversation with his loved ones and his environment that takes place as he emerges into his own personal consciousness. Here a language and an accent develop which will be indistinguishable from himself as a person, a "mother tongue" which will be his for life, a stride, a facial formation, and many of the basic postures which seem to create personality. These form his medium of expression; they lie in unconsciously formed patterns which shape the primary consciousness, and make him "Me."

Secondary socialization takes place when the individual enters a human community other than his native one. This is easily dramatized when a child enters school in kindergarten or nursery school. Here he encounters a different community of human beings, engaged in special tasks under the leadership of special functionaries, teachers, who are playing defined roles. The new student must enter into this secondary community in order to progress in his widening experience of human culture. He knows that there is something different here from his "mother tongue." First, it is something apart from himself: "out there," it belongs to a corporate group. He doesn't necessarily have to identify with it. He can play the role of a student and still keep a certain amount of objectivity in this new relationship. He can put on this uniform —student—and also take it off, as he wishes. He controls how much of himself he will allow to appear. He can keep the relationship quite formal, or open it up. In fact he finds it is usually best to use some wisdom in this just to guard his own private self from rude intrusion. He can "take home" what he wants from the experience. He doesn't have to have an existential relationship with the teacher. In fact, he rarely knows her apart from her role as teacher. That is usually the way he wants it. In fact, it is only possible to survive this experience by carefully guarding his primary consciousness.

Berger and Luckmann maintain that the proper balance of each of these types of consciousness and socialization is necessary for a mature growth of the human being. Simply to expose oneself in his primary consciousness to every demand of human life is to court emotional exhaustion. The feelings of man and his mind's capacities are not able to stand before such exposure. On the other hand, simply to play roles, actually to live within the secondary socialization is to be shaped by one's environment into a uniform mass. This is the fear of the younger generation as they grow up in a plastic, standardized world. It is easy to understand how they vigorously move away from socialization into their private consciousness.

It is our contention, with Berger and Luckmann, that the retreat into private consciousness is a great mistake. It leaves the System entirely in control of man's socialized consciousness, while one lives out his personal life in solitary moments of privacy. On the other hand, if we could develop a positive approach to forms of secondary socialization, if we could affirm anonymity as an opportunity that corporate life affords for the expression of our freedom as persons, we might begin to shape the System into forms that enhance man's life.

The Problem of the Structures

Of course, a positive approach to one's social consciousness pushes one into the problem of our structures and institutions. Some of us used to insist that there was a sharp line drawn through our culture—a line defined by those who, on the one side, affirmed our institutions and structures and were willing to work within them, and those who, on the other, were hostile to these institutions and structures and were eager to destroy them as soon as possible. That soon became an indefensible position, for no such easy line could be drawn. It became much better to talk not in terms of institutions, but in terms of processes, interactions, and participation.[4] This dynamic language transformed the structures and institutions into processes well within the power of human beings to use in shaping their futures. There are some who feel that the technological process has so escaped from the control of persons that we are confronted with a social life comprised exclusively of inhuman things. The horror of such a dream haunts us always, but the only positive approach to our dilemma is through those ways and means whereby we can humanize what we have. Having admitted this, we are in a position to look into the normal metamorphic stages of institutional growth.

Here again Berger and Luckmann are helpful.[5] For instance, John and Mary get married. No matter whether or not they accept the label, they now have formed an institution out of themselves. They are now an object of classification for others. They have a united system of meanings and pattern of actions. They now share certain processes of elementary life. How do they act? Well, first their previously acquired habits—their own primary consciousness —coalesce and become joint habits. Mary may notice strange aberrations in John which are slightly annoying. "There he goes again!" she will growl to herself, until she realizes that this is the way he *is*. Then she decides to join company with, "Here we go again!" A routine is thereby established. Out of these conscious adjustments and planned new actions, a web of routines is established. These routines, usually wound around eating, sleeping, washing, dressing, etc., actually provide real freedom for each partner. They relieve both of the daily task of decision-making and thereby free each person up for his own creative actions. At this stage of marriage, the experience can be highly liberating. Mary and John, thereby, have learned the basics concerning a social structure. Within these basics they should find freedom to develop their own skills, and locate the dynamics of authority. Their marriage is built by the interplay of these decisions and habits. How, then, does all of this solidify into institutional life?

Well, let's say along comes the baby. In anticipation of this event, the home is carefully prepared. Unless Mary has done this, her return from the hospital and the following days are chaos. Eating, sleeping, changing of diapers, yelling, feeding—all must be provided for; the couple is thrown completely out of phase unless routines become even more rigidly established. The increase in necessary duties brings about a corresponding increase in regularity which allows freedom for the individuals.

Thus, as the child grows up in a home, everything has its place. The freedom of decision of the first period is at an end. Necessities formulate the routines. Inasmuch as there are few changes, there is no visible sign of freedom to the child. "Everything has always been this way! This is the way things are!" is the child's feeling. Unless the parents can open up the space for daily choices or provide the processes for new decisions, a certain fateful feeling dominates the child's growing years even in spite of the affluence of the parents. In fact, it is precisely in suburban homes with wall to wall carpeting and furnishings throughout that the feeling of the closed institution pervades everything. No processes of change are evident. It is easy for children to feel that they have been shaped and destined to a life over which they have no control. The only thing they can do is resist as strongly as possible.

Of course the answer is for parents to work doubly hard to see that the freshness of the first stages of institutional life are always maintained. Manners there must be, but constantly changing manners with real understanding of what is intended. Routines are expected; they actually are necessary to free man for creativity. And this same sort of disciplined purpose applies to those hours of creativity in which we seek to attain new skills.

Worship and the Family

Several years ago at a national conference on worship, a Roman Catholic liturgist established the whole structure of the worship of the church on a family model. Using the father figure for the presiding minister, he built all he wished to say into this family figure. Of course one could predict the content of the question/ answer period. Sociologically trained Protestant clergy jumped on this model immediately. They reminded the liturgist of what was happening to the nuclear family in our culture, and to the father figure which had dominated it. The devastation was complete. The liturgist had no other model for the corporate worship of the Christian community than the gathered family under the father.

I have since pondered this experience long and hard. Try as I can, I find it almost impossible to imagine human community apart from the familial model. Certainly this figure is under attack. *The Death of the Family* proudly proclaims the end of the nuclear family and piles upon it the blame for just about every problem in human life.[6] Leaders of women's groups join in condemnation as they seek new forms of life.

On the other hand, persons in the university world are witnessing constant attempts around us at communal living. We see the first processes in the establishment of such institutional life. In many situations there is such resistance to ordered routine that everything is left to the feelings of the moment, and corporate decisions simply happen without anyone figuring out just how. As the group lives together longer, there emerge certain authority figures or patterns to lift the group above the tyranny of personal feeling. Until some such pattern eventuates, the commune is tied up in an endless whirlwind of discussion of routine matters while the movements for human betterment to which the communal living is dedicated suffer. These communes are experiments in uniting two kinds of consciousness-in-action: the primary consciousness which leads persons to express the deepest grumblings in their hearts, and the secondary consciousness which forces persons to perform communal roles for the sake of all. Some other name may develop for such communal experiments than "family," but one sees in them all the fundamental structure of family life. The great difference is clear: they have discovered the necessities of communal existence for themselves.

The congregation of tomorrow must provide for such self-discovery within its own program. That is a big order, for the depersonalization of human life is part of the system we have inherited. One can always count on spirited human beings to react vigorously to the violence done to their personal development by our highly organized culture, and that reaction will bring a serious distaste for all organized forms of Christian family life. We can already feel that distaste in the cry against all formality and the demand for unstructured and spontaneous "happenings."

But we are also gaining a modicum of experience in providing "happenings." The *disciplines* of spontaneity suddenly appear to be almost overwhelming. Corporate events just do not occur—the preparations for them are exhausting, the coordination of undisciplined persons is extremely intricate. Very few congregations can actually bring off more than a few "happenings" in a year's time. One begins to see that true spontaneity is developed by such regular disciplines as sensitize the whole person for the moment when he is needed.

Knowing this, the congregation must approach worship from its formal side. While sympathetic with the distaste of modern man for structures, we must put our emphasis on those forms with a sensitive program of education into worship. For it is through the tradition that we actually know who we are. It is through these forms that our revelation of God has come to us.

NOTES

1. See Abraham Heschel, *Man's Quest for God* (New York: Charles Scribner's Sons, 1954).

2. Ibid., p. 32.

3. See Peter L. Berger and Thomas Luckmann, *The Social Construction of Reality: A Treatise in the Sociology of Knowledge* (Garden City, N.Y.: Doubleday and Co., 1966).

4. I am indebted to Professor Karl Hertz of the Hamma School of Theology for this transformation of institutions into dynamic parts.

5. See Berger and Luckmann, op. cit., pp. 45–85.

6. See David Cooper, *The Death of the Family* (New York: Pantheon, 1971).

5   Language and
Liturgy

No doubt we are going through a period of the death and birth of language, one of the primordial features of human nature and culture. We have to become dumb before we can learn to use names and words faithfully again.[1]

Language is a central problem in our world, a shrunken world in which mass communication has brought foreign tongues right to our very door. The failure of man to communicate with man is evident in every event; the desperate need—before it is too late—for a common human language is only too vivid to our younger generation. We constantly reach for some sort of amplification and publicity even before we have anything to say, and this contributes to a language which is empty.

Members of the church are particularly jittery about the problem of language. We now seem willing completely to disrupt traditional language in favor of the immediate and dramatic. Our consciences are extremely sensitive toward those words that can recapture the NOW in the midst of our liturgies. First signs of this restlessness were when a few ministers operated on the *Thee*s and *Thou*s of the King James Version and the Prayer Book liturgies. But that helped not at all when the *dost*s and *doth*s and the *You who*s were left high and dry. It did provide stepping-stones toward other conquests. Next came changes in the theological content: we don't really believe in being "by nature sinful" anymore, the dichotomy between soul and body is no longer fashionable, the ancient creeds of the church no longer speak our language, etc. Then came a host of additional inserts which were intended to make benedictions relevant to the coming week, to confer blessings with a friendly personal tone, to free absolutions from any authoritarian connotations. We are helpless before such an onslaught.

These sensitive ministers were right in their general aim, for the problem of human language is primary for the church. If the church is to be the primary example of human community, then communication between human beings is of primary concern to all its members. But this primary concern for human intercommunication should set a different depth to the language problem. The church should not be fastening all its attention upon the self-conscious failures of its own language while ignoring the more basic problem of helping all men to find a common language, a language which will overcome loneliness, a language of true community.

Often the "tinkerers" are the very ones who merely irritate congregations which, underneath all the strange traditionalism of their liturgy, are managing about as well as one could expect. Meanwhile, the larger task of providing a human language for the whole community goes by the board. The psalmist speaks of the God of Israel as the one who puts the solitary into families—still a wonderful figure for our God. He is the one who takes the lonely man and places him in a truly human community where his tongue is loosed and he can speak. In a real sense, the people of God are placed in this world to be that family of God. A truly human language is therefore the deeply intended object of our efforts.

The Marvel of Speech

The philosopher Ernst Cassirer, when analyzing the wonder of human speech was attracted again and again to the life of Helen Keller, and particularly to that epochal struggle for a word which would open her life. That dramatic saga is told in the movie *The Miracle Worker*. The marvel of the word *water* drummed out to her sense of touch set this solitary person in the human family. When Amos Wilder suggests that "we have to become dumb before we can learn to use names and words faithfully again," he is imagining such a struggle for all of us in today's world.

When we return to the elemental level of the first word, we are amazed at the context of language. Such works as Edward T. Hall's two books *The Silent Language* and *The Hidden Dimen-*

sion[2] survey the bubbles which surround our own individual lives, predetermine our relationships, and provide for the space around us—all unbeknown to our conscious life. The spoken word is merely the ultimate evidence of a whole complex process.

It is the task of the poet to reach into this whole context of life —common to man—and bring up words meaningful to a community of men. To do this, the poet must engage the sympathy of other men by his use of images. The poet continually reaches out into the unformed, unconscious world and tries to form those images that can make that world available to man's whole self. C. Day Lewis has described the process:

> We may speak of the poetic imagination as the Holy Spirit brooding over chaos but it is still chaos over which it broods, and will remain so unless the poet's concentration is intense enough to elicit what is latent there. Or we may compare it to the dove Noah sent out, returning with a leaf on its beak: that leaf is only a token of life; there is still land to be won, and then the fire to light again, the house to build again, the old family's quarrel to smooth over again. For every new poem is, as Mr. Eliot has said, a new start; and at best it is but a tolerable substitute for the poem no one is ever great enough to write.[3]

The poet's task is done in face-to-face encounter. A poem is not to be pinned down in type on a page, but to be read out loud face-to-face where the poet's own manner and gestures and voice form the images, one after another.

Amos Wilder has described early Christian language as "face-to-face" speech, a language where one believer encourages another with his own voice, where commonly held events are retold and celebrated. In this respect Christian language took the form of poetry. Wilder does not completely equate the two, however, since the terms *poetic* or *imaginative* today suggest aesthetic or romantic categories whereas biblical language is a dynamic presentation of life's experience in the form of great pictures of God's life among us.[4]

The point is well taken though. Language in liturgy belongs to the medium of poetry. It lives in pictures, figures, and images which encourage empathetic effort. It assumes the presence of feeling within the congregation, and opens up vehicles with which that feeling can be expressed in definite actions. The language of liturgy is therefore *not* the language of the street or of everyday secular life. Whenever we try to make it a language of secular life, we are required to introduce some dramatic "happening," or to import the tremendous energy of the rock medium. But the development of feeling with words requires a different movement . . . toward the expression of fine feeling in common imagery.

The Nature of Liturgy

Having sketched the problem of language and the need to return to dumbness if we are again to discern the meaning of a true word, it is also necessary for us to understand what liturgy really is. Otherwise we will continue merely to have a number of gifted persons writing poetry, and foisting off their creations weekly upon a grunting congregation.

Louis Bouyer, a conservative Roman Catholic liturgist (formerly a Protestant) has urged a return to the basic sources of liturgy before we launch into wholesale experiments which actually destroy what we have:

> If the liturgy experiences deterioration through wear and tear, routine and sclerosis, it buckles even more radically under theories which owe it nothing, when people are trying wrongly to remake it in accordance with them. For here we are dealing not with those errors that are mere negligences or more or less profound insights. They are errors that are committed solemnly and on principle, and on the pretext of enrichment or reform they cripple and mutilate irreparably.
>
> Actually it is an established phenomenon that a liturgical theology which does not proceed from the liturgy, and finds nothing satisfying in it, soon comes up with pseudo-rites or aberrant formulas. Riddled with these, the liturgy soon becomes disguised if not disfigured. Sooner or later the feeling of incongruity in such a situation awakens a wish for reform. But, if, as is too often the case, the reform then simply starts from a theology that is in vogue at the time and not from a genuine return to the sources, it cuts without rhyme or reason into what is still left of the original and completes the incipient process of camouflaging the essential beneath the secondary. . . .[5]

The truth of this prediction lives, for example, among Christians who are at home in the college and university world. Experimentation in liturgy has been normal among us for a decade. A regular cycle can be seen: tinkering with the words of the traditional liturgy, injection of a new theology into formulas, substitution of poetry for psalmody and prayers, radical change of formal structure of the whole liturgy, substitution of "happenings," return to the tradition with a vengeance.

Bouyer forces us toward corrective study in the history of religions and depth psychology—studies which show how wrong we have been in our concepts of the development of religions.[6] We have an unerring tendency to separate words from their contexts, and thus we have assumed that liturgies have developed out of primitive sensibilities, from a time when man was overwhelmed by myths and superstition. Then gradually, as man developed, religion took on ethical dimensions and words were required to function only as important vehicles of meaning. It follows that, in man's advanced state, a religion of words is held to be the most elevated form of religious life. In the liturgy words become more and more important, and the liturgy itself from which everything developed is gradually left behind like a locust's shell.

Obviously this has been the path of Western Protestantism. Our services of worship have been crowded with words; worshiping has been largely an intellectual exercise. At this stage, however, simply to change around the words is further to confuse the issue and perhaps completely to erase the structure of worship. Even poetry is, today, an elitist solution and one which merely prolongs the end. For unless the shape of the *actions* of worship is rediscovered, the whole enterprise of worship will disappear.

Fortunately for us, the liturgical movement of this century arose in the midst of new discoveries in the natural sciences. Man's life no longer permits words to be isolated from their context. One can no longer make an easy separation between what is prophetical and what is mystical, consigning the latter to a time of man's infancy. The message of the younger generation is loud and clear in its discovery of dimensions of life of which elders have not been aware, in its distaste for the fathers' concentration on reason and words, of its new sense of human awareness and the critical need to put these insights to work before it is too late.

A Humble Example

Some years ago, this change of insight came to me in a homely sort of way. I was to preach one Sunday in a country church in the mountains of Appalachia. Knowing that there would be a small congregation and that there would probably be no love of liturgy, I simply prepared myself with a sermon, a prayer, and some general materials that could be shifted around for any occasion. Upon my arrival the congregation of about twenty-five had already gathered. It was a cold winter day and they were gathered around the pot-bellied stove. I went into a huddle with the elder and found to my surprise that this congregation used the liturgy of the church without variation. I was introduced to the organist, and off we started.

Well, we hadn't gotten far before I found this was going to be some experience. The responsories consisted in the clergyman's word and the replies of the congregation which the organist did alone as she pushed down and pulled up the keys of her instrument, all the while chewing gum. The congregation remained silently around the stove either listening or meditating. I came down to be with them for the sermon.

Afterwards, I asked how they ever introduced this liturgy to these people. The elder said that the congregation, being far away from the seminary and not having enough people for a pastor, could only get occasional seminarians to lead them, but these seminarians insisted upon the liturgy of the church. So they taught it to the organist and between the minister and the organist a good thing was going.

Now of course this was just the wrong approach to introduce a liturgy. One should have started at the other end. He should have started with those things which Christians *do* together: responding to the word, breaking bread, reading the Scriptures, and saying the prayers. From that one could then move to the liturgy itself.

Liturgy—The Actions of the People

I have often used a simple illustration to open up the actions in the normal Protestant service. Suppose you were a twelve-year-old boy who had, for some reason, received an invitation to visit a very great man whom you admired. How would you feel and what would you do? Well, first you would feel overwhelmed at such an opportunity, and would probably prepare yourself by buying a gift for the great man and wrapping it carefully. Then comes the minute when you walk into his home. You are met by someone who ushers you in. The hallway becomes much larger as you take each step and you begin to melt through the floor. Then when you are ushered into his presence, you blurt out some things you have saved up for this moment. Then he speaks to you words that you will always remember; you then give him your gift, and if he has a gift for you all you can do is murmur your thanks, pledge of service, and leave.[7]

In this very mundane sequence there are events common to human experience: preparation, entrance into presence with confession and absolution, your praise, his word, your offering, his offering (in the Holy Communion), your thanks, your service. And your service becomes the preparation for the next visit.

These actions happen to be roughly the succession of actions in our Western liturgy—the service. We have approached it psychologically here just to illustrate that the *actions* are not strange; in fact, granted the presence of God, they are extremely natural, belonging to the nature of man himself. That's the way we are, and that is the way such meetings take place. It is no wonder then, that the basic shapes of our liturgy have maintained this natural course of things.

We really have not thought of liturgy as actions, though. Give each of us the responsibility of leading devotions in a group and we automatically think verbally, not liturgically. We start by wondering what the *theme* shall be; then what materials might agree with the theme; then we string together a succession of materials that push the theme home. This worship is a man-centered, programmed effort at producing a result. But liturgy is something else—a natural action in the presence of God. Thinking liturgically, one would ask what action the people of God should perform in the divine presence. Materials should then be selected which get the people to act, perhaps the largest portion of time being spent in bringing them all together to the point of action. The action should then be performed. And the act is over.

To consider worship as a series of actions performed by the people of God is to have a great weight lifted from the words that are used. Action becomes the essential thing. One does not have to be so existentially intense about what one means if one means what one does. Consequently, whether one uses *Thee* and *Thou* instead of *You* is not the main question. That will depend upon what this particular people find most useful *for all to do together*. And this is the important point. The language of worship belongs to the whole people. Christian worship is corporate and its language is corporate. But such language presents us with a host of issues.

On the one hand, the speech of liturgy is a language of faith which each individual must somehow acquire for himself. "One must do his own living and his own dying." In this sense the whole language of our faith is basically one of primary socialization. It does not belong to the whole world at all. One cannot possibly secularize this language. It is specialized and refers to the experience of a certain community of faithful people. It requires the context of faith and gratitude even to exist. It is our "mother tongue."

The poignancy of the way in which we are intertwined in the peculiar accents of the language of faith is illustrated by a report on the habits of a group of West Indians:

> For all these people religion is so closely tied to culture, country and family that an intellectual approach or anything that would be called theology in modern language will not easily be heard. For a West Indian there may be a moment of intense reality even in a very infrequent Communion, and a nostalgic sense of "going home" in the words of a psalm, a hymn, a Prayer Book collect or a phrase of the Bible (A.V. only). He wants either deep emotion or impeccable respectability in religion and this is far more important to him than mere intellectual honesty. The poorer people of Barbadoes sometimes stand around the open windows

of their cathedral if they are not well enough dressed to enter the doors. But they will insist that the alms' bag be passed to them as they cluster outside. And God is not mocked.[8]

Would that some of our sensitive ministers could turn their antennae in this direction and hear the unconscious yearnings of some of their laity!

Primary or Secondary Consciousness?

In our last chapter we contrasted two types of consciousness: the primary consciousness which is our accent, our "mother tongue," our very own expression, closer to us than even our thinking about it; and our secondary consciousness which is the role we play, the robe we put on, the language we create for our public appearance. It is extremely difficult to say where the Christian language belongs for modern Christians. There was a time when the Christian accent was the mother tongue, when brothers and sisters were called by Christian names which recalled biblical scenes. Today there are very few Christian families left where the primary socialization of the family is in the Christian language, where the Scriptures are read aloud and commented upon, where prayers are said, hymns are sung, and a very natural bridge is present between normal speech and the Christian idiom. As a result the whole effort of Christian education has to be transferred from the family to the church. Yet the church, for most of us, belongs in secondary socialization—it is "out there." This means that the church's own family language has to be put on as a mantel, tried out for size. How much of it people actually "carry home" depends upon the quality of the teaching and the openness of the student.

At the same time, however, it belongs to the language of religious faith to be personal. It is naturally assumed that it belongs to primary consciousness. One must somehow make it existentially his very own. The only honesty imagined is that which belongs to this primary area. Secondary consciousness is ignored.

This throws worship, by nature communal, into crisis. Its language was *designed* to be restrained and objective *just in order to provide a common platform where people do not have to bare their souls.* Such an effort at corporate worship is held by many to be dishonest, and they attempt, vainly, to translate this corporate language into an appropriate primary form of language. In the whole process, one's own secular expression takes over in the name of worship. I fear that many of our present experiments do just this without facing embarrassing evaluations.

I would argue with Heschel, that the starting point for making sense out of the language of corporate worship is with the necessary idiom of corporate language itself, with what it is supposed to do, why, and how. We then can use this knowledge haltingly to *feel our way into* this language. Let us be specific and concentrate upon the language which we now use, English.

English Style

A good number of the Christian communions on the American continent have come from non-English-speaking traditions. As such, they have hung closely to their mother tongue long after settlement here, often for several generations. Around this mother tongue has accumulated a family context of cultural patterns which for many spells the life of faith. Adoption of the English language has been difficult for these communions. They have seen that English-speaking Christians have also had their own unconscious context of cultural life too, and they have been very chary of it.

Adoption of the English language has come for many as a necessity. But this simple necessity has not opened up for the neophytes just what they are adopting. They feel certain that something is changed but don't know what it is. This leads many to try to recover their lost feeling of warmth and closeness by changing words here and there, bringing everything home where it is cozy— even domesticating the Almighty.

Actually, the English have been known for their understatement, their love of institutions, and their corporate rituals. Indeed, their language—conveying some of these gifts—may be exactly what some of us need today. The English have developed a public language that is careful not to disrobe anyone, even before the Almighty.[9] Its language for public worship is a platform so open and general that each worshiper has the choice of what he will expose himself to. That is its primary purpose. Restraint, understatement, gracefully determined formalities—all in gentle candor —are certainly recurring characteristics of the English. Everything is in its place: for each type of concern, a proper expression. This seems to be the rule.

A very recent study, *Privacy and Freedom* by Alan F. Westin[10] seems to suggest that these English attitudes toward public and private life have much to contribute to all cultures in our technological, scientific world of 1984:

> Britain has what might be called a "deferential democratic balance," based upon Britain's situation as a small country with a relatively homogeneous population, strong family structure . . . surviving class systems, positive public attitude toward government, and elite systems of education and government service. This combination has produced a democracy in which there is personal reserve between Englishmen, a high personal privacy at home and private associations, and a faith in government that bestows major areas of privacy for government operations. There is also a tradition of tolerating non-conformism which treats much deviant political and social conduct as permissible private action. The balance among privacy, disclosure and surveillance in Britain is one in which disclosure or surveillance of associational and governmental activities occur less frequently than would be the case in democratic nations where the patterns of deference toward and trust in the Establishment were not so strong.[11]

Our intent is not to don the wig of an Anglophile. We are simply suggesting that Westin's point concerning the English people is also true of the English language.

Christian Honor

The traditional concept of Christian honor comes up at this point. When we ask in the marriage service, "Wilt thou honor . . .?" we are basing our question upon something which has almost vanished among us. To honor a person is to act in a way almost diametrically opposite what is usually urged in a psychologically conscious age. We assume that the way to closer human relationships is in unmasking and undressing, in taking off one's clothes and exposing "the real me." The currents toward such psychological unmasking are almost overwhelming today. Yet one hears significant voices protesting the analysis of one human being by another (unless a skilled person is helping a sick person back to health). The concept of Christian honor assumes that every human being has a certain walled-in area within which, with the help of the Holy Spirit in the church, he can find new springs for life. There is what Albert Schweitzer called a modesty of the soul which goes with modesty of the body. One does not climb into the secret thoughts of another—even of his beloved; but he surrounds her with deeds of love and then counts as precious those times when the walls are voluntarily lowered and conversation takes place. Faith in the power of the Spirit to move in the hearts of men and through community, is always prepared to wait for those precious moments to occur.

Robert Jenson has strongly argued the case for churchmen standing up against the present currents of psychological undressing, at least in respect to liturgical worship.[12] We should acknowledge the direction from which salvation comes: namely, from outside ourselves, from an audible message spoken in our midst, a message about what God has done in Christ, and from our own celebration of the audible message. To emphasize the *modesty* of the person is necessary today. Such modesty requires a certain reticence in public expression, a limited exposure, a large space within which one is not forced into revealing more than he wishes to reveal, but a space where commitment by voluntary participation is possible and probable. How essential this attitude is in public worship, some of us will just have to learn. It would not hurt us in America to learn through the careful use of the English language.

The Dilemma of Corporate Language

There is a further unexplored area in the church's use of the English language—the whole question of style. Stella Brook in

The Language of the Book of Common Prayer, has examined the form taken by English liturgical expression. She suggests that the language of public worship has a style all of its own because: (1) its corporate use requires a degree of objectivity; (2) it is used vocally by a group of persons, either said or sung, and therefore requires a rhythm which is easily mastered by a group; (3) it is used over and over again and must therefore have a rugged "wearing" quality; it is not properly a liturgy—a public rite—until it has been used enough to determine its survival possibilities. She suggests several modern efforts in translation where the result is successful, particularly this antiphon, a modern creation, used in compline:

> Save us while waking,
> Guard us while sleeping,
> That awake we may watch with Christ,
> And asleep we may rest in peace.[13]

The author goes on to hold that the language of both the Book of Common Prayer and the King James Version of the Bible gained immediate popularity and held it so long because they both emerged at a time when the spoken and the written styles of English crossed paths. It was also a time when the language had recently been enriched by French and Latin. On the other hand, Miss Brook asserts that today there is a huge gap between oral and written English which does not give much hope that within our time we will have mastered the problem of a fine spoken style.

Several years ago, I presented a study of the various biblical texts for psalms and chants for study. I was attempting to push us toward a choice of an official text for the Psalter which would spring our musicians loose in creative work—that is, after all, all they are waiting for. It came as a surprise to me that only three versions available at that time—the King James Version, the Book of Common Prayer, and the Jerusalem Bible—had texts which provided a rhythm suitable for choral speech, responsive reading, or singing. And there really was not much choice between the traditional language of the Authorized Version and the modern language of the Jerusalem Bible, despite all the furor for modernity in our churches. Since that time the Old Testament of the New

English Bible has provided a fourth alternative. The problem is clear: other contemporary versions did not envision the corporate use of the text, in speech or song, a most lamentable oversight since the simple recitation of the psalms is by far the hardest discipline to learn in corporate worship.

The style of a language sets the possibility for its corporate use, requiring a regular accent, and a memorable succession of words. These are necessary not only for a number of persons to use texts in unison, but also to assure longevity and wearability. For liturgical forms by their very nature are best used without the mechanics of reading; they are forms which the memory finds easy to retain as vehicles for action. Attention should center on the actions. This is a forgotten dimension in our rush for the new.

We have said enough now to offer some reorientation in our view of Christian worship. A return to the setting in life where a word-with-meaning is spoken is a return to a simple action within the context of responding faith. We do not underestimate the richness of this moment. All of the present rediscoveries of the human world of feeling and awareness are relevant if we are again to reestablish that moment.

Once, however, the actions of the people of God are seen as the building blocks of worship, a shift takes place. Language then accompanies the actions. Words do not carry such excessive weight as formerly. Attention should be centered on primary actions, then, and the people of God should be left with whatever familiar language can best get them to act.

NOTES

1. Amos Wilder, *The Language of the Gospel: Early Christian Rhetoric* (New York: Harper & Row, 1964), p. 9.

2. See Edward T. Hall, *The Silent Language* (Greenwich, Conn.: Fawcett Publications, Inc., 1959), and the *Hidden Dimension* (Garden City, N.Y.: Doubleday and Co., 1966).

3. C. Day Lewis, *Poetic Image* (London: Cape, 1969), pp. 68 ff.

4. Wilder, op. cit., p. 126.

5. Louis Bouyer, *Eucharist* (Notre Dame, Ind.: Notre Dame University Press, 1968), p. 8.

6. See Louis Bouyer, *Rite and Man: Natural Sacredness and Christian Liturgy* (Notre Dame, Ind.: Notre Dame University Press, 1967).

7. I have used this model in *Liturgy and Life* (Philadelphia: Lutheran Church Press, 1966) and *O Sing Unto the Lord* (Philadelphia: Fortress Press, 1966).

8. "The Ministry to Immigrant Communities," *Theology* (January 1969), p. 16.

9. Sec Stella Brook, *The Language of the Book of Common Prayer* (New York: Oxford University Press, 1965).

10. See Alan F. Westin, *Privacy and Freedom* (New York: Atheneum Press, 1970).

11. Quoted in *Encounter* (December 1970), p. 50.

12. The article was entitled "Orpheus, The Button-maker, and 'Real Community,'" *Dialog* (Winter 1971).

13. See above, n. 9.

Part III
ANALYSIS AND
SYNTHESIS

One brings to the concept "Christian worship" his very own picture born in his very own experience. Yet nothing in the church is as traditional as the content of the service of worship. It has grown up like Topsy through the years with no analysis of either its constituent parts or the rationale of their use.

Whole traditions of Christian experience in worship have been thrown together into this service. This process has been accelerated as Christian congregations have given up one after another of their other services, so that our services of worship are an amalgamation of rather different traditions which we have gradually gotten used to using.

We are attempting to take these strands apart, to look at each and open up its separate integrity and shape, and to suggest ways in which the tradition can be used to enrich the whole. In so doing, we find that there are actually four different traditions that are necessary in Christian worship, traditions which should be established for their own sake. Some of the other emphases which creep into our worship must then be separated and evaluated; these are necessary companions which enrich our worship and for which some place must be found.

It is intended that this scheme can actually be tried out by those who plan congregational worship. The year of fifty-two Sundays is long enough to provide opportunity for emphasis to shift about. A *whole* program for the congregation might evolve in which parishioners could achieve a better understanding of what they do and when.

6 The Christian Tradition of Worship

Throughout the Christian world today, a live conversation concerning the reform of worship sets up two opposing categories: traditional and experimental worship. It is assumed that everyone knows what these categories contain. Experimental worship is anything which is different from what we have done before. Traditional worship is, therefore, all that is not experimental. Usually the writers on experimental worship have had a very hard time with "traditional" worship, although they rarely describe this in detail. One must look behind each outburst against the tradition if antecedent events and factors are to be seen.

There are many of us, though, who have not had this traumatic experience with the tradition of Christian worship. In fact, we have found it so rich and broad that our present-day experience never fails to be deeply enriched through traditional worship. There is, for us, no danger of a lack of relevance in the tradition. As denizens of the twentieth century we bring all of the NOW with us as we worship: our awareness of world events, our success or failure in past days, the pangs of our conscience in an unjust and evil world. This NOW is then set within the perspective of the timeless and under the judgment of Him who is righteousness and mercy. It is therefore at times very difficult for us to know what some of these writers are talking about.

The truth is that few know what the tradition of Christian worship is in all its fullness. Our experience of the tradition is probably through one hour's exposure each week. Every one of us has become so accustomed to his particular Sunday morning worship as to be practically impervious to its messy character. In fact the word *worship* gains its content for each of us through the specific rite to which we are accustomed. The rite is so filled with all sorts of stuff that the word *worship* is no longer of much help. Thus, any evaluation of new materials and forms is quite impossible until we have reestablished meaning for Christian worship.

Standing in the 1970s and looking back through Christian history is like being at the wide-open end of a cornucopia. The various traditions of Christian worship have produced hundreds of forms and materials of superlative quality; yet all are dumped on us at once. With the successive erosion of one after another of the daily/weekly disciplines of Christian people, the remaining parts have been thrown together into the only remaining corporate discipline that Christians share: the Sunday morning service. It is as though all six courses of a banquet had been poured together into one great porridge and served to the hungry parishioner. Those whose taste buds have been trained for specific tastes at different times are the very ones we offend, while the untrained may find it all nourishing. Something qualitative is lost in the dish, at a time when the Christian's identity in the world is the one qualitative demand made upon him.

The Christian tradition of worship is like a large rope made up of many strands wound together. Each of these strands has its own color, its own requirements, its own character. When we speak of "traditional worship" we tend to lump together a good many different things.

A Practical Analysis

I think there is a very practical way to provide for some hopeful movement. It would be extremely helpful if each congregation would unwind the strands of the various traditions in Christian worship that are all knotted up on Sunday morning; then ask of each its source, its shape, its language requirements, its demands for space; then make hopeful suggestions for change. The results might look something like this:

TYPES OF WORSHIP	SOURCE	SHAPE	LANGUAGE	SPACE	SUGGESTIONS
A. Traditional Christian Worship					
1. The Word of God (Preaching)	Old Testament synagogue preaching service	assemble prepare listen respond	Scripture	what is needed to speak and hear	
2. The Eucharist (Holy Communion)	Passover Last Supper postresurrection meals	He took gave thanks broke distributed	of the family	room with table	
3. The Offices (Family Prayers)	synagogue early church monastics family life	psalms— imagery Scripture— tradition prayers	psalms or poetry Scripture— contemporary readings family prayer	anywhere	
4. Expression of Experience	prayer groups experience meetings pietistic groups cell groups	expressive of experience free	dependent upon medium	set up for occasion	
B. Auxiliary Activities Impinging on Worship					
1. Evangelism	early proclamation of Good News	free conversation	of the world for the world	in the world	
2. Program	American church	thematic	advertising	any space	
3. Education Into Worship	necessary to use forms	based on total program	instructive use	varied	

Here are seven quite different developments in our worship, each of which is subsumed under the word *worship*. Each of the seven has had its own history, origin, shape, language, and space requirements. Several *require* scriptural language, indeed, they are the bearers of Scripture to our day. They are the guardians of Christian identity. Another would seem to cry out for the language of the Christian family. Another opens the door for experiments in personal expression.

If this variety is characteristic of the worship we offer, it is equally true of the attitudes people bring to their worship. We have had enough studies of language recently to reveal many things that language attempts to do, provided the people using the language are aware of what is being done at each point. In these traditions there are several different ways in which language is used, and there is nothing to be gained in opposing one to the other if it is clear what is being attempted at the time. The language use for program is aimed at people-response; it is man-centered, with an exposed hook. On the other hand, the language use in the celebration of the word of God is already filled with meaning beyond our ken; the language use flows in the opposite direction here. To mix the two languages is to confuse the worshiper.

Again, the confusion of worship affects our architectural planning. Several years ago it was fashionable to build churches for eucharistic celebration—churches-in-the-round appeared all over the place with the altar in the center. This was a marvelous corrective, since we had assumed for centuries that the church is a collection of individuals on their pathways through life toward the heavenly places—a view which the Gothic floor plan exhibits. With the congregation gathered around the central altar, there is no escape from recognizing the importance of the *people* gathered around the holy things. However, this same treatment does immediate violence to the tradition of preaching, unless the preacher has his head on a swivel and a God-like voice. For preaching, or handling the word of God in the midst of a believing people, something else is needed. And maybe this takes more thought on the part of the architect than does the eucharistic celebration. After all, the latter can take place around any table, possibly in small groups which increasingly form the natural groupings of our corporate life.

A visual presentation such as our chart helps us to evaluate jazz as an expression of worship. We see that the term *jazz liturgy* is at best inaccurate. The term *liturgy* refers to the forms which the whole people of God use; the jazz medium is a subjective eruption of individual expression in which the members of the congregation of necessity start as spectators. Are not such jazz expressions akin to traditional meetings where Christians poured forth their own experiences and the listeners vibrated in response? Should the performers not be given this sort of setting to fully exploit their medium? No negative evaluation is involved if we insist that the jazz idiom really should have its own setting.

Evangelistic meetings in our churches have tended to follow nineteenth-century models—large halls, rhythmic songs expressing simple Christian experience, inspirational speakers. If this is what we have, we should call it what it is: large-scale prayer meetings to revive the Christian faith. True evangelism is testifying to the faith in the world. And this would be done much better in places where the world's life is shared: coffeehouses, rock groups, etc. Though some influence from these media will no doubt find its way into the congregation, the effort to turn Christian worship into a natural expression of the world's cries of pain is misplaced.

The Wholeness of Christian Worship

All seven of these different strands that make up Christian worship are necessary. It isn't surprising that all are thrown into one hour's experience on a Sunday morning. Yet this messy knot must be untied. Some place for the development of each should be found in the total program of worship for the Christian people. None can be ignored.

The heart of ongoing Christian worship is formed by celebration of the word of God, the Holy Communion, the Christian family prayers, and our expression of response. Elsewhere I have likened the regular use of these four traditions to playing a piece of baroque music.[1] Basic to baroque music is the running bass upon which everything—the jaunty melody and the harmonic enrichment—is built. Each unit is necessary for a satisfying piece of music. Christian tradition has assumed that its running bass is the regular use of the Christian family prayers—the ongoing foundation upon which life is lived; its melody is the gracious gospel of Jesus Christ as celebrated regularly; and its harmonic enrichment is the daily personal expression of Christian faith. The whole makes up the Christian liturgy, the actual service that the people of God render to him in the midst of their world.

We assume, of course, that *all* these disciplines are mixed with the world's life and its pain. That assumption is not too convincing to some of our Protestant friends who have had woeful experiences of worship far removed from this world, and who have consequently transferred the word *worship* to their acts of faith in the outside world. Though all of us are sympathetic to this intent, we cannot do that much violence to the whole tradition, fastened as it is to the life of God for man. We must assume that today the world is so much a part of us that there is little danger of a new pietism which withdraws from the world. Much more is there a danger of premature drowning by those who haven't learned the discipline of swimming.

Each of the elements in the Christian liturgy has its own shape. That is new for most of us. For centuries worship seemed to consist in a succession of various items, viewed from a purely verbal aspect, and strung together in some thematic whole, that is, confession, introit, Kyrie, Gloria in Excelsis, collect, etc. Only the rediscovery of action, of dance, of movement, of drama has brought out what should have been clear all along: that our worship consists of actions, and these actions are corporate. Louis Bouyer in *Liturgical Piety*[2] opened up the actions behind the service of preaching; Gregory Dix in *The Shape of the Liturgy*[3] performed a similar function for the Holy Communion.

The revelation of essential actions shifts the requirements for good experimentation from verbal reconstruction to those techniques which actually get people to do what they are supposed to do together. Thus the terrific weight which once lay upon the text is removed by concentration on gestures and actions. Imagination and movement carry much of the load, and when this happens, a strange shift comes about in our thinking about experimentation. Very often stuffy old words are pretty good vehicles for action, while brilliant creations of new texts simply dazzle people to a standstill.

Furthermore and in contrast to the fact that most of our approach to worship has been deeply personal, and that the experiments offered have been intended to open up personal expression, we must not forget that the platform of corporate life is made up of materials that hide rather than expose. *Only if people are sure that they won't be called to expose themselves will they take such part in corporate expression as to commit themselves to community!* This paradox needs more study by our innovators.

Only when one has accepted worship as a series of actions corporately performed by all the people does the essential need for an ongoing process of education into worship become apparent. It is inconceivable that we should pick all the fruits of the Christian tradition and make them into our bouquet for public worship, without knowing the least bit about each flower: its source, its roots, its growth, its maturing process. And *this* is the heart of our problem in worship—not making language relevant, or bringing the world into our space for worship.

Education Into Worship

So much that poses for experimentation in worship turns out to involve the actor-spectator relation. New liturgies are then judged by (1) their literary and musical quality as though they were pieces of art, or (2) their immediate effect upon the audience. Rarely is evaluation delayed until the new forms have become part of the people in their approach to God, like the old shoe of C. S. Lewis.[4] To become a beloved old shoe, a new shoe must be shaped by steps in daily life. This shaping of forms and liturgies is what we mean by education into worship.

It is a matter of some pride that congregations in America actually *do* the liturgy. Our European friends with their state-church support have long surpassed us in their music and art. Well-paid musicians are not dependent upon the democratic process. Europeans marvel, however, at our congregational participation. Their curiosity is aroused as to how we *do* it in America.

The answer is that we try to use every educational aid we can find. Of course the great danger is in turning worship itself into merely an educational experience. Usually, though, regular worshipers guard against that temptation, being slightly annoyed when prayers are disturbed by explanations and rehearsals.

There are those, to be sure, who maintain that liturgical forms that take explanation and training are far removed from the natural expressions of persons in our own day. Such forms, they say, utilize materials which assumed a much different background and require worshipers to place themselves into an alien world before they can worship. They wish to provide forms that are immediately available for the people, natural expressions of life. Actually, this is not true. "Happenings" require fantastic preparations and directions. Parish secretaries are busy for weeks before the event turning out proposals and revisions; deacons and cantors and lectors practice and make their suggestions; the whole "happening" usually comes off tardy, held together with scotch tape; the majority of worshipers still remain spectators.

The truth is that no corporate act can be performed without some training. When one has once accepted this fact as primary, whether this training requires a jump of the imagination or a plunge into the everyday world, is of little consequence. Education into worship is the important reality.

Family Prayers

The greatest crisis in worship lies today in the decay of Christian family prayers. Originally this was the tradition behind the Jewish synagogue's rehearsal of the great events of the past, reading the Scriptures, and praying. In the midst of these activities it was hoped that some miracle would happen, some unusual event by which God would reveal himself to man. This discipline was perpetuated and developed by Christian monastic groups into the offices where the communities carried on an incessant specialized ministry of praise, Scripture reading, and prayer for the *whole* church. Attempts were made by the reformers to keep the habit of such prayer, albeit in a shortened form. The heart of this observance went into the family prayer where the Scriptures were to be a source of daily strength. In our past tradition, the world of the Scriptures was a normal part of the Christian's conscious world; the Christian gathering on Sunday mornings brought together the thoughts that each family had been collecting. The Sunday lessons assumed this prior discipline, the prayers expressed it.

All of us know that this has eroded today, and with it the disciplines which formed the Christian character. Where the only exposure we have to the Psalter is on Sunday morning, the critical eye deals radically with every deviation from mature Christian faith. When all we hear of Scripture is in the chosen Sunday readings, its relevance to our changing moods is obviously questionable. When the only voice of prayer we raise is once a week, it is no wonder that the words don't come too well, and everyone leans on the prayers of others till the whole exercise is mechanical.

The Psalter has always been the source of the Christian imagination. In using the psalms we hang the picture of our past, in the midst of which we are able to give thanks. This is the setting for our life of worship—not the coldly secular world. If these particular pictures do not help our imaginations, then others must be found. But found they must be, and hung daily to create the mental space where we can worship the God of our fathers and remember what great things he has done. Without this memory, there can be no Christian man.

The Scriptures are the charter of our identity as Christians. They tell what it is to be a follower of Jesus Christ. They exercise an essential critical function, calling us away from our "relevant" hopes. Without the regular use of Scripture we can pretty well manufacture our own ideas of what our faith might be. It is not that the Scriptures contain all there is to our faith, no one ever claimed that. But they form the standard test of what our identity is as Christians, as the people of God in Christ.

Prayer is the breath of the Christian life. This is part of the way in which we participate in God's creation. We open ourselves up to his creative power. The tradition of praying for everything—dividing the whole into small pieces which can be remembered in an orderly way—is an essential discipline for stretching the Christian's heart and mind and uniting him with the world. Surely some place must be found for a revivification of this tradition.

Thus in a renewal of the disciplines of the imagination, of the Scriptures, and of prayer hangs more than in all of our popular secular liturgies. The fact that some Christians have found the life of prayer, newly approached, to be *the* way for them is evidence that much can be done. Our chief problem is that we are overwhelmed when we face the open cornucopia with its psalms, readings, and prayers; we have to start from scratch again. Perhaps we must initiate the essential disciplines which predated our family worship. This would mean a discipline of imagination, an opening to events which have brought us grace, a daily movement of mind and heart toward others. Within such a context we might reach toward that wonderful moment when all breaks open in a new revelation of truth.

In listing the seven strands which make up our program of worship, it is clear that four belong together: the preaching of the word; the eucharistic celebration; the offices; Christian expression. The first three make up "the liturgy" as contained in our service books. And the place for Christian expression has always been attendant to "the liturgy," sometimes officially encouraged, sometimes discouraged; it is, however, essential to make "the liturgy" live and to give it local color.

The other three strands—evangelism, program, and education into worship—are of a different character. We will argue that provision must be made for each within a total program of worship. We will insist, however, that the time and place for each is outside the space/time of worship as an act.

Despite the excitement of today's new forms, we have taken the position that another movement is necessary or Christian worship will just wither away. This movement is toward those disciplines that make up the Christian's identity in today's world. These disciplines are part of our unconscious life and are therefore hard to articulate, and thus it is that many church members are confused and silent in the face of changing forms.

The path to such experimentation as will move *the whole congregation* starts with taking these inarticulate feelings seriously, with analyzing exactly what we have in our churches today, with unraveling the strands of traditions, and with a free development of each of these strands in the hope of bringing together a new song to the Lord.

NOTES

1. See Henry E. Horn, *The Christian in Modern Style* (Philadelphia: Fortress Press, 1968), pp. 122 ff.

2. See Louis Bouyer, *Liturgical Piety* (Notre Dame, Ind.: Notre Dame University Press, 1955).

3. See Gregory Dix, *The Shape of the Liturgy* (Naperville, Ind.: Alec R. Alleson, Inc., 1964).

4. See above, pp. 3–4.

7   Preaching the
Word of God

The preacher, in an age of comparative enlightenment, when many of the persons he addresses in the congregation are as intelligent and as well-educated as he, and when they are accustomed to hearing, via television and community lecture halls, many speakers ever more intelligent than he, cannot hope to be relevant as a voice of authority, a bearer of *the* Word, or an ultimate source of wisdom and understanding. He cannot even pretend to carry off his act as an expert in the scriptures or theological inquiry, for, unless there is far more than that in his portfolio to manifest the importance of his opinions, most people today will not be interested: the Bible and theology are becoming daily more peripheral in their existence.[1]

With such an introduction, John Killinger describes the preacher of today as "a man, a sensitive, creative, poetic figure, grappling with the problems of being human and secular and whole in our time." He has accurately described where we are in American Protestantism today. His words are almost clichés by now. Things aren't what they used to be when the preacher was the best-trained person in the community, and people flocked to church for knowledge. Men have "come of age," as Dietrich Bonhoeffer has proclaimed, and they are no longer about to take the authority of any book or any man.

There is enough truth to these generalizations to convince everyone that it is all so. Certainly the Bible is not the constant companion of our people. Its authority over the life of the Christian is not immediately recognized. The ordinary preacher is not listened to with rapt attention.

On the other hand, I often think that it is preachers themselves who are passing around this generalization. Though all of these changes seem to have happened, the laity still come to the services of the church, appearing to listen attentively and wistfully to what the preacher has to say, hoping that he will not dabble in subjects where they are more competent than he, but that he will open up what the word of God may be. Despite all of the heralded changes, this is what they expect him to do.

Moreover, Christians just do not have any other charter for their identity. The Scriptures provide the authenticating seal of their integrity. Church and Scripture are intertwined in a life grip. It is extremely difficult to imagine what such a Scriptureless preacher really is.

James Smart takes just the opposite position in his book, *The Strange Silence of the Bible in the Church.*[2] He is appalled that at the very time when so much is known and readily available about the Bible the preachers are the most squeamish about using it. True, there is a very healthy problem of freeing the word of God from its imprisonment in a past age and allowing it to speak in our time, but never have there been better tools and helps available for the task. He urges a totally different direction of movement, toward the reestablishment of the Bible in preaching. For preaching, biblical study in the church schools, and the use of church libraries are the only ways in which the world of the Bible is available to the public in our time.

Of course, Smart's aim is to develop the Christian as one who lives in two worlds at once, the one always informing the other. The Christian is to be a truly modern man but also one who lives in the world of the Bible. He is therefore bilingual with all of the ambiguities and insights that such bilingual character provides. The current and crucial question before the church today is: Can we restore the bilingual character of the Christian layman in our day?[3]

To arbitrate between these two Protestant positions is difficult today. There are a growing number who would insist that the whole dimension of transcendence, necessary to Scripture, is foreign to us today; there are those who fight to hang on to the slim connecting thread between the biblical world and ours in the expectation that new depths will be plumbed. The currents are all with the former, for change manufactures its own publicity.

Another sign that would seem to confirm the declining emphasis on preaching is the mood of church architecture. In the past decades, architects have concentrated their planning on space which would be primarily used for eucharistic celebrations. The table seems to be the center, the congregation is gathered around it. Provision is made for some preaching, but that provision is obviously haphazard. The preacher is the first to notice this as he tries to project his voice in every direction at once. It is easy then, for Roman Catholics, warm with *aggiornamento* affection, to speak positively of the "homily" again, believing thereby that they have come a long way toward the Protestant sermon.

Many of us are extremely happy that the Roman Catholics have rediscovered the disciplines of actually preparing sermons on the basis of scriptural texts. However, the homily is hardly in the tradition of Protestant preaching of the word! It is just too bad that the reunion of Catholic and Protestant had to come at a time when the Protestant pulpit had sunk so low. For we have a great tradition of preaching the word of God. Our services of the word attest to this; the centrality of the pulpit has meaning to the Protestant. Of course there were great excesses in an overconcentration upon verbal services where everything was talk (or hymns for relief). One can understand when many of our writers react against their dour past. But there was much more . . . and much that should be restudied before we throw out the baby with the bath water.

In a very perceptive address, Professor Heiko Oberman once opened up the context of original Protestant preaching.[4] He showed how the three great reformers, Luther, Calvin, and Zwingli, actually transferred the Roman Catholic concept of the Eucharist to the preaching of the word of God. The reformers found great difficulty with a church which could ascribe automatic effect on believers in the reception of the sacrament because of the presence of Christ, but actually they transferred this very concept of the presence to the preaching of the word, and believed that when the word is preached in the midst of a believing congregation, Christ is automatically present and the effects are immediate. Most of Oberman's hearers had heard the Reformation rhetoric, but we are all used to treating it as merely that. Oberman forced his hearers to see that the great reformers actually believed this, and then posed the question as to what the preaching of the word in the Protestant tradition might be *without* the concept of the presence.

Posing this question divides the answerers into two camps: on the one hand are those who automatically answer that we naturally do not believe in such a presence anymore, and, therefore, the living context of Protestant preaching is nonexistent and we should give up the tradition; and on the other hand are those who are stimulated to wonder if there is not much more to the preaching of the word than meets the eye. What if one really believed that there *was* a presence acting while the words were proclaimed?

Until recently the argument between the two answers would narrow down to whether one was a mystic or not. If one believed that there was more than met the eye in the activity of preaching, he was called a mystic. It was then assumed that the average man was a pragmatist for whom such mystical nonsense was useless.

New Discoveries

In the past decade, however, studies of human communication have given us new platforms from which we can see ourselves. We have come to the end of a period of visual communication, of book learning, of the printed page. Ever since the Reformation, we have tended to get our information out of books. The presence of the dispenser of the information was unnecessary; words are made timeless in print. One could no longer detect voice, gestures, personal presence except by an empathetic leap of the imagination. Information was impersonalized.

Of course, with the advent of radio and television, this visual age came to a close and now we are again affected by the personality of the informer. Because of this change, we can now see our concentration upon a visual, bookish, culture as having been restrictive, screening out personal interchange and spontaneous understanding. We are now beginning to understand a little more of the context of a preliterate culture.[5]

The Reformation was such a preliterate culture. Despite the use of printing to spread the gospel, the bulk of the people were illiterate. They were entirely dependent upon the oral presentation of information. In this way they were cousins of biblical people, and they understood the Bible as belonging to an oral culture.

Once one places the Bible and preaching in a preliterate, oral culture, all sorts of recognitions suddenly jump out. If one is presenting a message orally, time suddenly becomes an essential factor. One can only hear spontaneously—now—or he misses it. The accent, the emphasis, the gestures, the general demeanor and presence of the speaker are all important if we are to judge what he is really saying. The attitude of the group within which he is speaking, and their response are esssential ingredients in the total message.

Studies of surviving oral cultures, particularly their folksong tradition and even their preaching,[6] have brought forth intensely interesting insights into the form and structure of their presentations. Thus commitment to memory of huge batches of materials require formulas for recall, structures for telling the story, rhetorical exclamations for audience participation. To tell the story becomes a community act and the speaker becomes a common actor with the audience. The whole action is a community celebration.

Surely all this is implied in the Protestant tradition of preaching. This tradition, moreover, merely recovered an essential discipline that belonged to the people of God in the Old Testament. After all, Luther was primarily a scholar of the Old Testament. His immersion in the Hebrew text allowed him to escape the hardened world of traditional Old Testament teaching of his time and discover anew the world of the Old Testament.

Louis Bouyer in our day has rediscovered this same world. In his *Liturgical Piety* he discovers the discipline of the *Quahal,* the called community, of the Hebrews coming together at the behest of the leader, preparing themselves with appropriate actions, listening attentively to what the leader would say to them as the word of God, and responding with their offering, prayers, and their service. He finds this rhythm of actions recurring again and again until it actually becomes the succession of actions in the synagogue service, the ancestor of the Protestant "preaching service."

The Oral Word

Some of the essential reverence for what happens at such a gathering is revealed by Martin Buber in his description of the oral presentation of the Scriptures in the midst of a believing community:

> The text was intended to be read aloud. The translators did not merely want to translate word for word, but to convey a rhythm that would do justice to the use of the pericopes in the original. They were not meant to be read silently, as we have been normally reading since Augustine's day. The original way of reading was to recite aloud, and where the text was read in a religious community, it was lightly intoned, almost sung. That is one of the reasons why the text is not an easy one for people nowadays who flit past day after day. Of those words only a quintessential—or supposedly quintessential—few remain as ideas in the mind. When the written word was something rare and therefore very precious, it was pondered over and over again. The activity of reading was more what we today would call "close reading." It was not at all a matter of flitting cursorily through page after page *ad infinitum* and trying somehow to digest them. But it was with such "close reading" in view that the text of the Holy Scriptures was put into book form and so handed down, and the task of a good exegete, is to read again, as men used to read when writing was a youthful and meaningful art, a progression of spellbinding texts by means of which the soul of man could journey forth into the uttermost reaches of time and space. The runes of the divine revelation are the vehicles of a mystery still more profound—something to be deciphered rather than read and heard.[7]

The Scriptures of the Old and New Testaments are continually best sellers. This seems to be rather miraculous compared to the use they get in most homes. Yet the presence of the Bible in so many places is not what will extend its power to ages to come. That power is found in the midst of believing communities where expectant people listen while its words are proclaimed orally, turned over and over for meaning, and applied to our day.

ANALYSIS AND SYNTHESIS

John Wilkinson sums this up in these words:

> The clearest pattern, therefore, is the reading and public exposi-
> tion of the Scriptures in the liturgy. For here the Christian
> community is visibly present, the very community in which the
> Spirit gives life, in which God's word may have free course and
> be glorified. The Bible from its place of honour, is read to all the
> community together, so that all may hear the literal sense, and
> receive the words of the men and God who write them. And when
> the reading is complete and in the Creed the community has
> expressed the context of its belief, the appointed teacher of the
> Church presents the application of the Scripture. No presentation
> of the Church's task of interpretation could be more graphic. No
> better preparation could be devised for the offering and receiving
> the Body and Blood of Christ.[8]

In the Protestant tradition, the churches are divided between
those that set forth assigned readings for the church year, and
those that give this choice to their ministers. There are problems
with each system. Certainly a fixed order of readings often fails to
intersect with the most crying needs of the day, it can lack relevance. On the other hand, the choice of lessons by one minister
drops him into the pit of his own preoccupations and "hang-ups."
A well-considered cycle which projects the life of our Lord and
the Christian life which evolves from it is probably best. Relevance
is expected in the presence of the twentieth-century man who must
expound Scripture—the preacher. Some of us who have been
going through the cycles of the church year for decades can attest
to the surprising way in which we have been opened up wide by
texts which, at first, seemed to be irrelevant. The actual presence
of fixed texts over against us have brought forth that energy, and
that responsiveness which alone can proclaim what might become
the word of God.

Presence

And what can we deny about the concept of presence? Again
and again there has been a tremendous *plus* above all that we have
done or said, which has formed the community into something it
wasn't before. There is nothing especially miraculous in this plus

90

if we believe in God. The Hebrews talked about the *shekinah,* the shadow or presence of God which comes when the community gathers around the word of God. The claim of Christ, "Where two or three are gathered in my name, there am I in the midst of them," is nothing but association with that *shekinah,* that presence.

There is a graphic portrayal of this concept of presence in the Western liturgy. When the Gospel for the day is read it is preceded by "Glory be to thee, O Lord" and succeeded by "Praise be to thee, O Christ." Within the Christian tradition, the congregation stands for the reading of the Gospel; in some congregations the official representative of Christ in that place comes down the aisle to read the Gospel, and is greeted by these verses. The intended aim is clear. Christ is present in the reading of the Gospel, and the congregation greets his hidden presence.

Now there are two ways of dealing with this action. One can rationalize the language and do away with this quaint custom, the way most of us go in changing our worship. Or one can stretch his imagination. If we are surrounded by enthusiasts who wish to stretch our human awareness by all sorts of techniques, how much easier to project our imaginations to dimensions which we have as yet not plumbed?

The same can be done with the sermon itself. Certainly each preacher should stand before his congregation as a man of their time and place. That is sometimes impossible to do in a high pulpit. Each step up into the pulpit separates the preacher from his people and makes him removed and distant. On the other hand, some of us have found that each step toward the people brings down their defenses and unites us with them. The preacher should be free to try various styles for various occasions until he feels perfectly at ease with his people. For this reason, I would favor providing many places from which one can speak—possibly with a movable pulpit or lectern.

On the other hand, the preacher should have a vivid sense of the presence of Christ "in, with, and under" the words he proclaims. Possibly it is good for him to ask himself as he prepares, "How does Christ come to his people in the lessons for this day?" That would simplify and sharpen his preaching. It would also

91

provide the quiet pastoral tone that is needed to be a sympathetic leader of Christian people in this world. This type of preaching which recognizes the presence of Christ with his people can be called "sacramental preaching." It seems most appropriate in services where preaching accompanies the celebration of the Holy Communion.

Of course this is not the only kind of preaching we are called to do. Meditative preaching is closer to the homily, but is also based on a scriptural background. Again, the presence of the preacher on the same level with his hearers increases the likelihood that all will consider the sermon a commonly shared investigation. Where one accepts the place of preaching in the midst of the people, opportunity for discussion and comment in the midst of the presentation is clearly present.

On the other hand, there is still place for expository preaching and topical treatment of relevant subjects from the pulpit. In both cases the presentation has to be much more formal and suitable for the pulpit. Indeed, the congregation will expect a well-thought-out treatise if a preacher walks into the pulpit. There is enough tradition behind this presentation to create the habit. Protestant congregations over the years have probably gained a good deal of their knowledge of the Scriptures just through such preaching. It is by no means dead, as the conscientious preacher of today can testify. Congregations yearn for a good exposition of what the preacher thinks is the word of God for that day.

The Protestant tradition of preaching, therefore, holds within it much more than meets the eye. A simple revivification of a biblical homily by Roman Catholic priests is the first step toward our tradition of the word, but only the first step. One of the dilemmas which follows from the increased celebration of the Eucharist at the main Protestant service has been the decrease of emphasis on preaching of the word. The liturgical movement, arising from Roman Catholic churches and centering around the Eucharist itself, has had little that is new to offer on preaching. The result is often negative toward the word with less time and energy going into sermon preparation. It is merely the preparation for the main event, the celebration of the Eucharist.

We have said enough to maintain that preaching has an honored and special place in our Christian and Jewish tradition; that through preaching the people learn the world of Scripture; that in cooperation with the preacher they handle the particular words in the presence of Christ; and that through this corporate act they are made into his body. It is time to reestablish this tradition and to demand from our preachers a very high valuation of their homiletical task.

Listening

We have not said much about the hearers. And there are certain disciplines for the hearers that bring them into the action of preaching. These disciplines are quite visible among some Christians. Recent studies of preaching among some of the Southern Negro sects have opened up the way in which congregation and preacher work upon each other until the finished product is far beyond what either could have hoped for in the beginning.[9] Amens and Hallelujah responses are only the most vocal signs of this empathetic cooperation—the congregation and preacher get worked up together and the Spirit takes over.

In our staid congregations very little happens this way. However, we do try to provide sung responses to oral presentations. Scripture reading is always followed by psalmody, verses, songs, or hymns. They are intended as meditative responses to what has been heard. One thinks of the cow, after chewing a tuft of grass, meditating over the taste by chewing the cud; this is the purpose of such responses. They are to insure a corporate handling of the word of God, the creation of a responsive and empathetic community within which ordinary words can become the word of God for this community.

Now we are beginning to see the importance of the service of the word for the Christian congregation. The whole action belongs to the whole people as they try to discover what God is saying to them through their meditations on Scripture in the midst of their praise and confession. To think corporately of this task is to escape the authoritarian "hang-up," the picture of an authoritarian preacher proclaiming the very words of God to a fearful and unthinking people. That sort of proclamation *has* left us, but it never was the whole concept of Protestant preaching. It lacked the context of presence. Now, having rediscovered the broad context within which preaching has its intended place, Christian congregations can work cooperatively with their minister in devising disciplines within which the Scriptures can come alive in their midst. The service of the word of God has an honored tradition among us and an exceedingly bright future in our new world.

NOTES

1. John Killinger, *Leave It to the Spirit* (New York: Harper & Row, 1971), p. 156.

2. See James Smart, *The Strange Silence of the Bible in the Church* (Philadelphia: Westminster Press, 1971).

3. I have argued for this bilingual stance for the Christian in *The Christian in Modern Style* (Philadelphia: Fortress Press, 1968), chap. 10.

4. Heiko A. Oberman, "The Preaching of the Word," *Harvard Divinity School Bulletin* (October 1960), pp. 7–18, especially the following: "I should like to suggest that the genius of the Reformation is best described as the rediscovery of the Holy Spirit, the present Christ. . . ."

5. See especially Walter Ong's *The Presence of the Word* (New Haven: Yale University Press, 1967) and Amos Wilder's two works, *Theology and Modern Literature* (Cambridge: Harvard University Press, 1958) and *The Language of the Gospel: Early Christian Rhetoric* (New York: Harper & Row, 1964).

6. See especially Bruce A. Rosenberg, *The Art of the American Folk Preacher* (New York: Oxford University Press, 1970).

7. Quoted in M. A. Beek and J. S. Weiland, *Martin Buber: Personalist and Prophet* (New York: Newman, 1968).

8. John Wilkinson, *Interpretation and Community* (London: Macmillan, 1963), p. 231.

9. See above, n. 6.

8   The Eucharistic Celebration

The liturgical movement of the twentieth century has been almost exclusively a eucharistic revival; in every Christian community there has been a revival of interest in the Holy Communion. The breaking of bread has been reemphasized as a celebration of joy by the people of God. Congregations have moved away from four isolated celebrations a year into weekly celebrations. Parishes that had small weekly celebrations have moved the Eucharist to the place of honor—the main service.

When churches start to move in this direction, there are no arguments that can hold them back. The traditional reservation of the Holy Communion for crisis occasions, preceded by long preparation, necessarily withheld the sacrament from people as a daily food—one cannot stand many such crises in a year's time. Considering the serious preparation for the sacrament that was necessary in our older pieties, the provision of four celebrations a year was probably all that a human being could take.

Confession and Communion

Movement toward a weekly Eucharist was impossible as long as the Holy Communion was surrounded by a crisis mentality. This is an inheritance of our Western Christianity in which confession and the necessity of cleansing before receiving the sacrament has a long history. In fact, in our immediate tradition confession and communion are inseparably linked. The dour countenance of the conscious sinner still hangs over our eucharistic celebration even when confession itself has been removed from the event. It is extremely difficult to break through this piety with a smile.

It is not hard to see, though, that our traditional communion liturgies contain two quite separate moods: that of contrition, and that of celebration. It was not difficult, therefore, for scholars to show us how confession and the Eucharist were originally quite separate. Once we knew that, we were able to separate them and allow each mood to dominate in its own place.

There was a time when rural congregations used to have a separate service of confession for the congregation on Friday or Saturday before their communion celebration on Sunday. Though in a restless society this is not possible, many congregations have taken the hint and have separated the act of confession from the celebration of the Eucharist. Sometimes this act of confession precedes the service as a sort of voluntary prelude; in some congregations, private confession is available for several days before the celebration.

Once the confession is removed from the actual service, a joyful celebration can take place. The emphasis then shifts toward the celebrative eating and drinking together of the people of God. Reemphasized are the bread and wine as representative of the things of this world, and as tokens of people who themselves celebrate. Bread baked by families in the congregation and wine similarly prepared are brought to the altar as the offerings of the people. The petitions for the people's prayers are also brought forward as part of their offering. The whole celebration has undertones of a family covered-dish fellowship supper in which the chief guest is the Lord himself. The celebrative mood is reminiscent of the pristine joy of the early church in the presence of the risen Lord.

United with this revival of the Eucharist is a vivid identification of the Christian with the created world through the bread and wine. It is assumed that the things of this world brought to the altar—the bread and the wine—symbolize the whole secular world in its distress. The bread that is broken is the Christ who was broken for just this world. The distribution of the bread and wine is a distribution of Christ's gifts for this whole world. The dismissal from the table is a commission to take these gifts into that world.

The Shape of the Actions

This whole revival is based on solid scholarly grounds. Chief among the scholars responsible for this movement was Dom Gregory Dix. His *The Shape of the Liturgy*[1] uncovered the structure of the first prayers used by the church in the liturgy. He showed that they were prayers used at the time of the offering and consecration of the bread and wine. They had a structure which actually duplicated in pantomime the actions of our Lord at the Last Supper: he took the bread, he gave thanks, he broke the bread, he distributed it. These actions then became the structure of actions in this prayer of thanksgiving: offering, thanksgiving prayer, breaking the bread, distributing the elements. They also become the unseen structure of the liturgy itself.

Though Dix's positions have been attacked on scholarly grounds, his main position remains solid even today. Perhaps the biggest discovery has been that though this pristine prayer of consecration did maintain a constant structure it was also at this point in the service that the presiding minister broke into free prayer for the congregation. This has provided an open door for modern enthusiasts to go poetic and create hundreds of eucharistic liturgies and prayers which are now in circulation. Meanwhile, liturgical scholars try to bring us back to the basic structure of the eucharistic prayer for our regular celebration, believing with Dix that something fundamental to the meaning of the whole Christian life is at stake right here. This structure is as follows: thanksgiving for our creation and redemption, the remembrance of the Last Supper and the words of institution, the prayer for the Holy Spirit, prayers for the church.

Essential to the whole liturgy is the retention and repetition of the orderly actions of our Lord: taking the bread, blessing it, breaking it, distributing it. To fasten one's mind on these actions while belonging to the body of Christ in this world is to be conformed into the pattern of his life. It is to be made Christian through the Eucharist.

Eucharistic enthusiasts assume that, once the liturgy is cleaned of its confessional hangovers, the actions become clearly visible and the people immediately understand what they are doing. They also assume that because they are handling earthly stuff in a natural way, everyone will get the message: the Eucharist deals directly with our social and cultural context. The man who receives the Eucharist often is the man who is always actively engaged in problems of human distress.

Both assumptions, however, fail. Many of us have cleared up the service till the actions are clearly visible. But the symbolic act of eating and drinking as the children of God is at depth accessible only to an empathetic imagination—and that is a rare item today. The whole sacramental act is, frankly, strange to a people who are largely the products of a rationalistic, scientific culture. Moreover, though the whole movement of the Eucharist is toward this world of bread and wine and people and events, something happens among us that keeps us constantly celebrating and rarely plunging into the world. If frequent celebrations actually developed Christians who are broken for the world, then one could shout that this is the way in which the church could be reformed. Something is still lacking, though.

We must admit—after a decade or so of pushing for frequent celebration of the Eucharist—that misunderstandings cloud this revival. The first is in the connection of confession and Eucharist. Perhaps it was necessary to separate the two for a time. The dour cloud of gloom had so permeated the celebration that even the word, celebration, was out of place. But "celebration" by itself gave rise to a whole movement toward the secular. Coming at the time when Protestant theology had just freed itself of transcendent connotation, this new celebration took on all the trappings of a secular "happening."[2]

Celebration

The rediscovery of the celebrative character of other cultures against the serious, purposeful Western culture; the new understanding of play and its place in life's fullness; expanding awareness of movement, sensual sensitivity, and new means of expression; multimedia expression—all this happened within a few years. The eucharistic celebration became the vehicle by which in the church such exploitive media were employed. Today everyone is for celebration! But when this type of celebration is poured into the forms of the Eucharist, somehow it doesn't come off as one would hope. Everyone has a wonderful time, but no one knows just what standards there should be for evaluation.

There is a real movement in understanding, though, even among the most radical of innovators. In the early sixties the movement to the Eucharist was a wonderful step toward freedom for American Protestants. Overwhelmed by their Puritan heritage with its torrent of words and absence of life in worship, they readily jumped to the celebration of the Eucharist for relief. An almost total deafness to sacramental language in their own tradition gave the new movement a freshness that was a totally new thing. Within this medium people could finally celebrate their own humanity. The Eucharist was primarily an expression of a new freedom in which many identified closely with the biblical desacralization of man and nature. Man and the created world were allowed to stand in their own right.

That can last for just so long. Then one must ask positive questions about what one is doing. Besides being a celebration of freedom, a human happening, what else is the Eucharist? And at just this moment a new understanding of the specialized character of certain times and places in human life became a gracious vehicle. Huizinga's *Homo Ludens*[3] was the first in a series of books that projected human *play* as such a specialized time/place. In order to play, one has to set aside a certain time and space within which one will do certain things according to certain rules and for a certain period of time. By creating such a separate time/space, one could—without dealing with the transcendent character of the Christian life—bring back time/space for the whole tradition of worship, but still in secular guise.

Of course, the missing element all along had been that of confession. In operating on our traditional linking of confession and the Eucharist, we had actually done more than we had intended. For confession is a natural response of man in the presence of God even at the time of celebration. True, there needs to be some separate treatment of confession, including private confession, and new ways to express corporate confession without clouding the whole world with one's penitence. But behind the need for confession is the recognition that one lives one's personal life in the presence of God; and under the need for corporate confession is the recognition that the people of God have been charged with responsibilities that they do not fulfill. The whole dimension of creaturehood as recognized in the presence of the Creator had dropped out of the celebration of the Eucharist. In our antipathy to what we considered to be cheap Victorian reverence in an imagined place of God's presence, we had dealt savagely with the whole attitude of creaturely reverence.

One could have expected the Roman Catholics to be of some help here. Generally, however, newly freed priests and nuns have been too enthralled with their secular freedom. They have run with the free churchmen, often passing them on the first lap in their rush for human happenings!

Festal Celebration

Among the various current reconstructive figures for new meaning to the Eucharist, I have found that of Frederic Debuyst most helpful in *Modern Architecture and Christian Celebration.*[4] While still agreeing that Christian worship is basically celebration, he is more specific and identifies the Eucharist with festal celebration. This still keeps the figure within human experience, for we all have our special feasts. But a feast is something very special. Involved in a feast are:

—a special value which one wants to celebrate with his friends
—a kind of aesthetic exaltation which involves all the preparations
—the invitation of special guests, their placement for the maximum communication
—a grace expressed in variety of female dress and orderliness of male dress
—festive conversation
—a succession of carefully planned stages in the feast which will move toward the special value

—an expressed affirmative Yes will be voiced to the whole created
world
—the end will be planned just right to send the guests home with
the value communicated to them

This description of a festal celebration provides an extremely
homely figure which any of us can fill in from his own experience.
We know that the feast is something special, something expensive,
but that expense is part of the essential character of the event. We
prepare for it carefully: we plan who is to sit next to whom, how
the conversation will begin, what will be served, and when to
bring the feast to the climax. The feast "breaks up our normal
pattern of time and space, opens a window in the wall of our daily
life and invites us into a world where the rules, the conventions
and the values are new and different."[5]

It does not take too much thought to realize the difference that
a festal celebration as a model makes in worship. It brings us back
from an indiscriminate celebration of anything human to the stated
value that forms the celebration. One cannot help but remember
that our Lord constantly referred to the messianic feast, and used
many illustrations from his observations of what goes on at a feast.
Of course this is what has been preserved in the celebration of the
Eastern church. At their Divine Liturgy the people of God have a
foretaste of the messianic meal; they imagine themselves tempo-
rarily in heaven ahead of time. Such an imagined model invokes a
reverent mood.

Debuyst uses the festal model to set the Christian celebration
within the whole tradition of the people of God:

> All the qualities which constitute the human phenomenon of the
> feast—sublimity and grace, freedom and harmony, superabund-
> ance and order, together with its spirit of unanimity, universality,
> recapitulation of the past, anticipation of the future—have to be
> transmitted here into the concrete shape of the Christian celebra-
> tion, into the paschal climate of its setting. Assumed, transmuted
> and perfected also through the Eucharist must be the dynamic
> power of the Jewish Passover: the passage from slavery to free-
> dom, from sorrow to rejoicing, from mourning to festivity, from
> darkness to light, from servitude to redemption.[6]

He argues that the church building must be the place

> where God's family meets to obey the Lord's command to follow Him, through His atonement, in the sober, strict, transparent, luminous, peaceful, active, deeply human reality of the new creation. This is what must be seen in the words "Paschal meeting-room."[7]

Our Jewish Background

This opens up a totally different direction for human rediscovery of celebration, namely, through opening up for Christians their Jewish background. The celebrations of Sabbath and Passover have been totally misunderstood by Christians over the centuries, yet both are basic to our liturgies. We have been disappointed to discover that the way back to understanding of our own tradition is not through Western liturgists, schooled in Roman Catholic practice, but through the unashamedly human liturgies of our Jewish brethren. Though the reformers rediscovered the Hebrew Scriptures and through them the prophetic principle, we went only halfway. For the Western liturgies still locked us within one particular tradition of Christian life—a tradition which had deserted the celebrative actions of worship for clerically performed actions and words, and which had mixed confession and celebration into one piece.

In this day when we react against any sign of the transcendent or supernatural in our language or action, it is well to remember that our Scriptures come out of just such a background. Pronouncing the name of God was abhorrent, impossible to such men. One could never see God face to face. Only his glory, his *shekinah*, his Name could be known by man. Every indication of his reality had to be discovered through the means that had been given to man. Nothing else was available. But in, with, and under the whole of the created world is this reality whom we haltingly name God our Father. It follows, then, that our celebrations of his presence will center around those specific events and places where knowledge of him comes with greater clarity.

Such an event for the Jews is the Passover, a celebration of freedom for new responsibility as the people of God. Such an event for Christians is the Pasch, the second Passover, freeing us to announce the transformation of the whole world through Jesus Christ, our Lord. These are the values we celebrate.

For many of us from an older piety, all this is perfectly all right. But we had been trained to believe that the fundamental value in the Holy Communion was the "forgiveness of sins." Where is the forgiveness of sins in the new celebrative rite? When confession and celebration were separated, did this emphasis merely melt away?

Actually it didn't, but in many liturgies this is no longer important. In the intense desire to get away from a medieval individualism where we completely forget that our liturgy is the act of the whole people of God, we tend to jump over all individual emphases. Our traditional celebration tended to be a very private action without the slightest contact with other persons. The very title *communion* was a misnomer. To correct this misunderstanding perhaps we went too far. The announcement of the forgiveness of sins is not only an individual assurance, it has always been the pronouncement of the presence of the kingdom now, in the power of the Spirit. We belong to a people which has experienced the forgiveness of sins, and this is an essential part of our proclamation of the Good News. Therefore, even in the most celebrative and joyful parts of the liturgy, we should proclaim this forgiveness.

Perhaps the issue is that traditionally most of us thought so exclusively of the Eucharist from the viewpoint of confession that we transformed the *whole* celebration into individual confession and absolution. We never went any farther. Our piety remained privatistic and obsessed with the need for perpetual cleansing. We never ventured on the other side of forgiveness into the life of the people of God for the world. As a reaction against this type of pietistic failure, perhaps we are now moving too far away from the forgiveness of sins as an essential part of our proclamation. As this is brought back into a central position as an announcement of the presence of the kingdom and of the power of the Spirit, we will introduce a new mood into our present celebration. That mood will be one of creaturely awe and humility. Those voices who now set forth the spirit of play as the mood for eucharistic celebration may keep that model, but they will surround it with the spirit of respectful children in an entirely new world of power.

The Presence of Christ

We haven't said anything as yet about the presence of Christ in the Eucharist. We should give thanks that the long hassles between Christian communions about the means of this presence are now at a new stage. Lutheran and Reformed, Roman Catholic and Anglican have come to a general understanding that we are talking about a presence during the entire activity of eating and drinking. This avoids the endless arguments about the ways in which Christ is or is not present in the actual bread and wine, and greets him as the Unseen Guest in the celebration.

It also restores some of the character of the celebration of the early church. Dietrich Ritschl in *Memory and Hope*[8] has done us a great service in reviving the concept of *Christus praesens* as the center of our theology. He shows how the static concepts of God as Perfection, All-Power, etc., in Augustine's day actually removed from us the power of God in time and space. We no longer thought of him as a powerful presence, but moved him above time and space into some ethereal area. The whole concept of the risen Christ with his people becomes a bit of history then; it inspires us to the degree that faith can be nourished by a backward glance over the historical shoulder. The Lord-to-come is postponed till the end of time—an obviously far distant time by our way of thinking. The ideal of such a Christian life lived between the event of the Gospel and this end becomes that which climbs to the "beatific vision"; sainthood is the state where this becomes reality.

For Ritschl the missing dynamic in this description of the Christian life is *Christus praesens,* always hidden and therefore giving life to Christian worship instead of being just a principle in Christian experience. Ritschl attempts to restore *Christus praesens* to the center of theological reflection. Then theology becomes reflection upon the life of the people of God centered around this Christ-on-the-way-to-becoming Lord—reflection upon the process by which that which is hoped for comes to be. In so doing, he gives theological argument for the weekly celebration in that presence. It is this *Christus praesens* under the forms of proclamation and celebration that enlivens our faith and inspires our hope. In other words, the saying of Jesus, "Where two or three are gathered together in my name, there am I in the midst of them," is really true every time we celebrate the Eucharist just as it is pictured in the postresurrection gatherings of the disciples with their risen Lord. This presence, still always contained in the rhetoric of every Christian communion, is the object of our imagination when we celebrate the Eucharist. In so doing, we actually recreate his life and become his body in the world through his grace.

The Eucharist, therefore, contains the explosive power for a revolutionary way of life. If it is genuine, it should mix with the suffering of the whole world. The enthusiasts for frequent communion have seen this clearly. Sometimes they actually insist on a worldly setting to emphasize the point. We can agree with their intent. Unfortunately the rhetoric here is not the same as the act.

Though congregations throughout the world are finding new life in the restoration of the weekly Eucharist, we must admit that the forms and spirit of that Eucharist we seek are most elusive. Enthusiasts should be tempered by our present failures; they should not promise what cannot yet be found. Simple multiplication of eucharistic celebrations is not the answer. Only intense struggle will lead us toward knowledge of just what we are doing, and of how our celebrations can involve us completely in our "liturgical service" of the world.

NOTES

1. See above, p. 83, n. 3.

2. At this writing, Harvey Cox is in the midst of this celebrative emphasis. He is probably doing a great service for us all in celebrating where we cannot go and with people we cannot reach. He does not, however, propose that his experience should be ours.

3. See Johan Huizinga, *Homo Ludens* (Boston: Beacon Press, 1955).

4. See Frederic Debuyst, *Modern Architecture and Christian Celebration* (Richmond, Va.: John Knox Press, 1968). Reprinted with the permission of the publisher.

5. Ibid., p. 12.

6. Ibid., p. 19.

7. Ibid.

8. See Dietrich Ritschl, *Memory and Hope* (New York: Macmillan, 1967).

9 The Family Prayers of the Church

There is an overwhelming tendency abroad to romanticize man. The search for the essential human element within each of us, has led us to expand the possibilities of our awareness. We know that each of us is conscious of only a very small portion of life. In the enthusiasm to reclaim the areas of human experience lost to us, we are apt to ascribe to man inner powers which are just not there.

I remember a conversation with a very dear Quaker friend in which I envied him and his community the ability to listen and respond to the prompting of the Spirit. That has always seemed to me to be a practice which lies just this side of heaven. I need all sorts of crutches to pull me out of myself and into a common concern. He responded sadly that something was happening to this gift in Quaker circles. Many of the meetings, unable to carry off the old traditional Quaker meeting prompted by the Spirit, have set up evangelical services not unlike those of other Protestants.

Upon further questioning, he stated that the cause of the departure of the Spirit from the meeting was probably due to the dissolving of a scriptural context. After all, the Friends were men and women of the Scriptures. They lived the Scriptures at home and taught them to their children. When they came to the meeting, they did not just come out of all context and expect the Spirit to move within this vacuum. But they came prepared by their disciplines of Scripture reading and prayer, expecting others to come in like fashion. The meeting merely gathered up what those, prepared by this context, were led to say within a corporate context. The meeting was considered to have been successful if from this cooperative contribution came a common concern. Therefore, when the whole preparatory context evaporates, there is little from which the Spirit can speak. Rigid formalism takes over.

107

This was extremely instructive to me. For most Christians find themselves in the same position. For centuries it was always assumed that daily praise, Scripture reading, and prayer would be the normal activity of Christians—their regular natural breathing within the kingdom of God. Each Christian congregation, it was assumed, would establish its own order of cooperative praise, reading, and prayer. It was then assumed that Sunday worship would gather up the praise, reading, and prayers of the whole congregation. Members would come prepared. The liturgy would contain praise, readings, and prayers but they would really be shorthand for what the people were already thinking—symbols to point them imaginatively to pictures, images, and petitions.

Once one cuts away this context for congregational worship, the language on Sunday morning has to carry a tremendous weight of its own for which it was not designed. Unimaginative reformers cut away the shorthand and the pictures with great rationalistic scissors. The result is usually a text which has immediate relevance to the week's happenings, and all the dangers of partisanship and lack of judgment by the leader are rubbed in with salt. This is unfortunately where we are today. Little emphasis is presently placed on restudying the whole tradition before permanent changes are made. Instead the movement in experimentation has already gone from wave crest to wave crest beyond recall.

In the hope that there are a good number of congregations that are serious about reestablishing habits of praise, readings, and prayers, the tradition is presented in this chapter. Certainly all Christians, individually, are conscious that they have not been able to keep up private practices of praise, reading, and prayer. It has been assumed by most of us that this duty was a purely private one, a matter between ourselves and our God; and we have asked his forgiveness often.

It comes as a surprise to us to find that this expectation of each Christian of private devotions is at best a recent one; that for centuries the church did not expect each Christian to be able to perform this by himself. Instead, praising, reading out loud, and praying has been a corporate action of the whole family of God. There is a good source for this: in the Jewish family and synagogue practice where the heads of the families led their families in psalmody, Scripture reading, and prayers. This was the ongoing conversation between God's people and God.

Christians took over this synagogue practice without much change. After all, why change since our Lord and the disciples prayed thus? There is some evidence that the early church was given to this practice. However, with the rise of monasteries, these offerings of praise, readings, and prayers were handed over to a specially trained and disciplined group of monks who performed this service for the whole church, leaving the ordinary layman to his Sunday observance. In Western tradition, these offices (for so these services at various parts of the day were called) became the function of "the religious" or the clergy. Every church member could know that corporate prayers were being offered every hour of the day somewhere in the world for him. By intention, he could join in.

At the time of the Reformation with its emphasis upon the faith of each individual, this system of clerical prayer obviously had to be revised. The reformers provided a morning and an evening service (matins and vespers) for families and congregations. Each preserved the structure of the office tradition: psalmody, Scripture reading, canticle, prayers. In Protestant tradition they have been used by several communions as congregational services, often on Sundays. Family use has been spotty, almost nonexistent. From time to time there are romantic recoveries among committed Christians in a sort of communal gathering. For such gatherings shortened forms of the traditional offices have been provided for each three-hour interval of the day. Recently the students of one denomination prepared such a series and it is used constantly for church meetings throughout that denomination.

But with all these sporadic revivals it cannot be said that the praise, Scripture reading, and prayers have been reestablished as the prayer life of our Christian people. Perhaps we can no longer think in terms of such formal orders in our time-scarce age. Maybe we will have to take the order apart, see what is involved in each act, and then suggest ways and means for providing this ingredient in the life of every congregation.

Praise—Psalmody

When all is said and done the critical problem of language in worship for us today lies in the use of the psalms. Our whole tradition in Jewish and Christian worship has been through the medium of the psalms. Psalms have formed the language of the saints and mystics before us. Practically our whole religious vocabulary is derived from the Psalter. The influence of this collection of Hebrew poetry cannot be measured. Our Lord himself cannot be understood without some knowledge of this language.

Frankly, though, there are very few Christians who are motivated by this language. Most assume that it is strange, irrelevant and not worthy of effort. The most faithful laymen will often surprise their minister by admitting that, after decades in the use of the psalms, they cannot understand what it is all about. Seminary professors can count on student response if they ridicule liturgical use of the psalms where picture language is vividly used, for example: "Save me from the lion's mouth, and from the horns of the unicorns." Of course no one has seen a unicorn, but maybe the dilemmas in the face of the unseen and imagined are as great as the obvious ones like the lion's mouth.

In the middle are a good many Christians who, while not objecting to the use of the psalms as a whole, are very anxious to have rigid editing. They feel that we should have gotten beyond expressions of violence against one's enemies, especially in the Christian church. Yet where we have edited the psalms and left out many from our service books, a change in the spirit of the age brings those left out into favor again. I remember discovering that it was Psalm 73 that sustained our Christian brothers in prison under the Nazis when that was one of the psalms left out of our American edition.

Among the most energetic innovators in worship, the psalms are no longer popular. Poetry has taken their place, and poetry which is much closer to our day. Of course there are booby traps in the corporate use of poetry. For most of it was not written for corporate use and lacks the obvious accents that would bring the people together as one voice. Certainly some sort of corporate poetry would be a proper substitute for psalmody, granted its content centered on the relations of God and his people. We would urge, though, that these innovators actually study the psalms themselves in worship—how they are used, what techniques are necessary for their congregational use—before they attempt to replace them.

In the face of such negative feeling toward the psalms it would seem unwise to even give them another look. However, there has been a significant restudy and recovery of the psalms in congregational use throughout the world today. Perhaps the best-known recovery was by Father Gelineau in France. Using the most recent discoveries of scholars of the psalms' background in liturgical congregational worship, Father Gelineau translated the psalms into a memorable rhythm, provided very simple choral progressions to the rhythm, used solo and chorus plentifully, and provided instrumental accompaniment, hopefully with percussion instruments.[1] These settings, translated into English in the Jerusalem Bible, have been used in many of our churches with joy and a sense of accomplishment. They give a totally different view of the psalms as songs to be sung with movement.

A very interesting, though unknown, effort by Richard Hanson called *The Psalms in Modern Speech*[2] tries to provide the actual Hebrew rhythm in the English medium. The various psalms are presented in their probable vocal setting. Thus choir, cantor, and congregation all have their own place and their own lines. Our traditional use of printing the psalms for responsive reading treats them all alike; Hanson provides great variety for interesting experiments in congregational response.

These are but several of the many new translations which are offered us today. All of them have sprung from the exciting discoveries in psalm research of the last decades. They open up a wide area for experimentation, and one which can bring rhythm, movement, instruments, and the warmth of children into our worship.

The use of the psalms is to awaken the imagination, to hang pictures around our space for worship in the midst of which we can worship our God. In some ways we are too serious in our present usage. We assume that each word is the worship itself rather than the means. Traditionally, sitting was the position for the use of the psalms—a sort of preparation of the heart for one's own worship. Richard Hanson has described what the psalms should do for us in worship:

> When we consider the broad span of time covered by these one hundred fifty familiar psalms, we realize that our fingers are feeling the pulse of a people, for here is the heartbeat of faith that was born out of a long and continuing experience with God. Here are reflected the great moments of Israel's history, both triumphs and tragedies, and here is the daily fare of continuing worship. In this one collection of psalms we can trace every significant moment of Israel's history: the Exodus and the birth of the tribal league under Moses and Joshua, the gradual conquest of the promised land, the rise and development of all the beliefs and hopes which centered in the God-chosen kings of the Davidic line, the many victories and defeats and crises of the Israelite kingdoms, the fall of the North, the fall of the South and the shocking experience of the Exile, the return to Jerusalem, the dreams and toils that went into the building of the second temple, and the various trials of living as a little religious community in a big world of powerful kings and nations.
>
> This is more than an interesting collection of ancient literature. It is a multi-voiced credo, the response of a people to the Almighty God who led them with stern kindness on a journey they never quite fully understood. To read the psalms is to bear the risk of being moved to prayer and praise, to join these people in their confession of faith.[3]

Professor Hanson almost persuades us to ask him for the chapter and verse references. Then biblical history could be learned by song in our church schools.

Underneath this recital of great happenings is a way of life—a way which looks earnestly and expectantly for the unusual, the miraculous in daily life, the moments when suddenly Reality breaks through and grabs a people. Over and over again the psalms shape this expectant posture, celebrating the great experiences of the past and opening one up to immediate experiences in the present. This discipline of expectancy provides the context within which something *can* happen. Therefore it is of tremendous importance.

We were almost persuaded that the psalms were foreign to us till Father Gelineau stimulated the movement of recovery. Now their use will be as wide as the existence of congregations with programs of education into their use.[4]

If worship is the Christian's use of poetry in the midst of the world's prose, the psalms are the imaginative tool by which the poetic mind is developed. They are essential in freeing the imagination.

The Reading of the Scriptures

In the Western tradition of the offices it was provided that the Scriptures should be read through in succession at least once a year. It was assumed that the Christian should know his Scriptures because those writings point to the source of Christian self-identity. If I understand Erik Erikson aright, a person caught in an identity crisis finds that identity by examining his origins and history in the light of the immediate future.[5] Through this process he solves the crisis by becoming certain of the space for his future.

We should remember this in our use of the Scriptures. We should not expect that they would be immediately relevant to the present. That is not their task. But they do tell us who we are and where we have been. Moreover, they do point us to dynamics in the present which lead to our future. As such they are a tremendous aid in our search for our identity as Christians. Because what we are today is of immediate relevance to any situation, sometimes the Scriptures can actually provide relevance in depth. A popular Bible study technique of our student days was to read a passage, passing over all those parts that we could understand until we came to a part that was just crazy. This is the exact point at which we should center our attention, open ourselves to the text until the strange world of the Bible—not our own—speaks to us in a way that challenges all that we are and have been. That deeper relevance becomes the final direction for our movement.

Basic to our openness to Scripture is the Christian's position that his life is not created by himself but is received from God. Gerhard Ebeling has underlined this viewpoint toward life:

> Man's true freedom consists in his receiving himself from else-
> where, that he does not owe it to himself that he is, that he is not
> his own creator and thus cannot free himself from himself. . . .
> For it is the mystery of human personal being that it is summoned
> from elsewhere, that it exists in response and as response, and that
> therefore man is wholly himself when he is not caught up in him-
> self, but has the real ground of his life outside himself.[6]

The Scriptures do not define the whole territory from which man
receives his life. They are only that part which defines his origin
as a Christian, and which provides him with the living dynamic.
But this is enough to make them important to his life.

Every Christian should have some familiarity with the Bible.
Most of us try to gain this privately, reading silently from time to
time. This is no substitute for having the words read orally. In the
chapter on the preaching of the word we described the importance
of this oral reading. The words come alive in the telling! In fact
even the translation we use is an imaginative interpretation of the
original. Again Ebeling tells us of Luther's aim in translation:

> However cautious we are, we must not forget that these are the
> words of one who spoke to his own time what it needed to hear,
> words uttered with the compelling force of what can be uttered in
> the light of the day, with the liberty of one who is completely
> absorbed by what he has to say, and with the practicality of one
> who is hitting the nail right on the head. His word is drawn from
> holy scripture and inspired by it alone. It is equal to the over-
> whelming task demanded by the scriptures of translating them
> into the language of his own age in accordance with the principle
> that he himself laid down for the interpretation and exegesis of
> the scripture: "You must ask the mother at home, the children in
> the street and the common man in the market-place, and see on
> their own lips how they speak, and translate accordingly, so that
> they understand it and realize that you are speaking German to
> them." The holy scriptures and the present day intersect as it were
> at a single point, in the conscience that hears the word. It was
> Luther's concern that the word of God should be heard in this
> way.[7]

We will recall the similar efforts of J. B. Phillips which have produced a paraphrase version of the New Testament as well as the

version by Clarence Jordan, *The Cotton Patch Bible*[8] with its partisan view of the Southern scene. Certainly every congregation should have some planned reading program going from season to season, using whatever translations or paraphrases are best suited to its people. In the liturgy of the church I would stick to accepted versions. In the family prayers of the people of God, I would urge any approach which seems to be advisable.

Several years ago our students, constantly irritated by scriptural passages which they did not understand, asked that secular readings be substituted for, or added to, the appointed scriptural readings. For a short period we attempted to do just this, using them as additional readings. Most of these readings were excellent passages of written prose, but they were meant to be read and they suffered greatly when proclaimed in a congregation of persons who were listening without the text. By comparison the Scriptures seemed to be of an entirely different style. On the other hand, the study of these sections in small groups was immediately possible and of great help. On the basis of such experiments, we would urge that collections be made by the church of possible readings, and that such readings be provided as settings for Scripture. Often such a reading becomes an excellent prelude to the worship of the day, or a comment on the Gospel for the day.

We are entirely in sympathy with those who wonder if we always have to reach back several thousand years for our present guidance. A great effort is demanded of the church in the direction of living in the present. We think that this point has been established now; that the movement toward experimentation is toward providing just such materials; and that a contrary movement toward deeper appreciation of scriptural disciplines must attend the revival if our identity crisis as Christians is to be resolved.

Prayers

Kornelis Miskotte has created two aphorisms which stimulate our thought about prayer: "The world is the realm where there is no prayer." "Prayerlessness is indicative of a fundamental loneliness."[9] The presence of God and conversation with him is what makes the religious man. That conversation is his religious breathing, his life itself. And because "our God is the God who puts the solitary in families," this life of conversation is one among other believers. Prayer is and has always been chiefly a characteristic of family life.

The whole family used to order the prayer life of the total family. In the tradition of the offices, each office was assigned certain times and places to pray for and about. The provision of these services throughout the day, every day, meant that the worshiper was reminded of the whole world, and he offered his prayers for it.

When this structure fell apart, the ordinary layman was given no substitute. Not having been taught to pray with regularity, he found himself conscience-stricken before the heroic demands of the church upon him. All the corporate demands for prayer, now left without fulfillment, were thrown at him. He was supposed to pray for everything, remembering everyone—and do it all the time. Huge visions of prayer lists and large blocks of time set aside were just too much for most of us. In the face of such heroic demands we just stopped praying. After all, our private prayers couldn't be that important!

Lacking between the church and the layman was a congregational plan that a whole group could perform. Today one of the most amazing signs of change is found among Christian students who have revived prayer groups and speak with great enthusiasm about them. They are simply organizing that middle group—that Christian family—which can read Scripture and pray. Congregations might well take note.

Once order is established for daily prayer, then the whole task of prayer can be divided into reasonable units. On successive days one can remember the church, the nation, the state of the world, the world of culture and industry, families and the home, all conditions of men, those who have gone before; or perhaps successively: daily work, the nation, homes, reconciliation, the suffering, the church.[10] Some such schedule for the whole congregation would be all that is needed to encourage many members into a program of prayer.

Style of Prayer

Perhaps the place where style is most noticeable is in prayer. All Christians have been taught to pray at some time. Prayer is not a natural activity. Each of us has learned to pray within a certain style of language. We are immersed in this; it is our "mother tongue." It really doesn't matter whether we use *you* or *thee;* what we first learned is natural.

When we read about Jesus' teaching about prayer it becomes evident that we are much too "uptight." He evidently went far beyond the stylized synagogue prayers of his day. He dared to open up his heart in his own expression. He urged his disciples to address the Almighty—the unaddressable—as "Abba," the beloved title for Father. Thus the simply expressed prayer is always a direct aim of Christian expression.

Corporate prayer, however, is much more encircled in a stylistic tradition. The early Christians naturally adopted the rhetorical style of address current in the Graeco-Roman world. This style is still preserved by the Eastern Orthodox church in its liturgies. The content of prayer is packed with biblical imagery, and each prayer is almost a recital of the acts of God in the past. Beyond this the prayers are filled with abstractions characteristic of Greek philosophy. Long subordinate clauses were part of the oratorical style of that day.

In the Western church, we have followed a different path—that of the Latin style. In contrast to the Greek style, the Latin style was terse and compact, almost a contest in trying to compress whole sentences into compact phrases in memorable Latin. The characteristic paradigm of this style is the *collect*. Its form has influenced the way in which the Western Christian prays and the collect is the model prayer of the whole Western tradition. Generally stated, the collect is divided into five parts: an address, an antecedent reason for the prayer, the petition itself, the desired effect or outcome, and the formal word of praise. Safeguarded within this general form is the heart of Christian prayer. For as Jesus reminded the Samaritan woman, we do not launch petitions toward an unknown God but to the God we know. Our prayer is based upon what He has revealed about himself in his mighty acts. When the collect form fastens upon this revelatory act of God, we may be sure that the prayer will be answered.

The antecedent reason is the hinge upon which the heart and mind of the prayer is fastened. Stylistically, this antecedent reason is expressed in our English translations by a relative clause. Again and again we pray, "O Thou, Who . . ." which in the fervor toward replacing *Thou*s with *You*s becomes the infamous *You-Who* absurdity which convulses our people. Most new approaches to the collects recognize their essential value as compact packages for the mind and heart. They assume that today we no longer use relative clauses but instead speak in separate, short sentences in a most direct manner. Therefore the new approach to the collect utilizes a series of short sentences, although it does retain the general structure of the collect. This would make the Latin scholar weep for it does violence to the passion for economy and terseness. Yet for those of us who have been trained through the use of the collect, it appears to be a usable bridge toward finding our own expression. We will doubtless still prefer a great many of the well-known collects in their wonderfully memorable forms.

Those most active in experimenting with new forms of prayer which can involve the whole congregation have taken up the litany form and exploited it far beyond its usefulness. Litanies should preserve their stylistic origin. They were intended for processional use in days before people could read. A trained cantor would recite and then the whole congregation would respond with acclamations and short prayers that were easy to remember so that they could respond while keeping their attention upon the whole activity. The modern provision of elaborate, wordy litanies in mimeographed form transforms movement and oral response to silent reading and occasional involvement. Sometimes the writer of the prayer gets carried away and actually gives long paragraphs for the congregation to read. He not only misunderstands the litany form, but he forces the whole congregation into choral reading—a very difficult discipline that no one has really learned, and one that is not exactly conducive to natural public worship. The creator of a litany should always bear in mind that it is a responsive procession. Every attempt should be made to provide easily remembered responses which actually keep the congregation involved in the whole process.

It is very encouraging to see such Christian communions as the Episcopalians and the Roman Catholics attempting bidding prayers, litanies, and general prayers which no longer assume that a congregation of people can listen to more than a paragraph or two at once. Various techniques are used to provide responsive actions which really involve all in the prayer. They are gratefully received by a people who know full well how rarely one can focus one's concentration and how much help is needed to become involved in a corporate act of prayer.

Psalms, Scripture reading, and prayer—these regular disciplines joined together to nourish the context of Jewish and Christian piety. It was out of this nourishing context that the prophetic voice sounded; it was within this context that our Lord lived his life. One can sympathize with those who today find the style of the language quite foreign to their everyday experience. However the underlying intentions of each of these disciplines are fundamental for the religious life. If the psalms are not themselves used, then the symbolic pictures which they provide must be created in another way; for the imagination needs their stimulation. If the exact words of Scripture are difficult, stories of men and women of faith must be told to surround us with the community of believing people. If prayer forms from the tradition no longer serve as living vehicles for our own expression, then the church must provide its own ways to open up the expressive outpourings of its members. Imagery, reliving the experience of faith, and conversation with the living God are the necessary context for Christian life. One cannot count on individuals to provide this for themselves. Its provision is a part of the church's task in every locality. The church's liturgy must enlarge itself to accomplish this end.

NOTES

1. The Gelineau Psalms can be procured in two volumes of thirty and twenty-four each and in recordings from the Gregorian Institute of America, 2115 W. 63rd St., Chicago, Illinois 60636.

2. See Richard Hanson, *The Psalms in Modern Speech* (Philadelphia: Fortress Press, 1968). Reprinted with the permission of the publisher.

3. Ibid., vol. 1, p. x.

4. See below, chap. 12, for some of our suggestions toward this end.

5. "The young person, in order to experience wholeness, must feel a progressive continuity between that which he has come to be during the long years of childhood, and that which he promises to become in the anticipated future; between that which he conceives himself to be and that which he perceives others to see in him and to expect of him. . . ." Erik Erikson, *Insight and Responsibility* (New York: Norton, 1964), p. 91.

6. Gerhard Ebeling, *The Nature of Faith,* trans. R. Gregor Smith (Philadelphia: Fortress Press, 1961), p. 115. Reprinted with the permission of the publisher.

7. Gerhard Ebeling, *Luther—An Introduction to His Thought,* trans. R. A. Wilson (Philadelphia: Fortress Press, 1970), p. 58. Reprinted with the permission of the publisher.

8. See Clarence Jordan, *The Cotton Patch Version of Paul's Epistles* (New York: Association Press, 1968), and *The Cotton Patch Version of Luke and Acts* (New York: Association Press, 1969). The records Jordan made reveal this version as an oral one; the sound of his voice is really needed to establish the provincial ring.

9. Kornelis Miskotte, *The Roads to Prayer* (New York: Sheed and Ward, 1968), pp. 16 and 17.

10. I have set down two possible structures for daily prayer. One can construct his own.

10   Expression of the Christian Experience

After a most discouraging proclamation of the doom of Israel because of its apostasy from its covenant Lord, the prophet Hosea imagines that great day when perhaps reconciliation might become complete. He imagines the final completion of man in the return of the people of God with their own offerings of words as the sacrifice of life: "O Israel, return unto the Lord thy God; for thou hast fallen by thine iniquity. Take with you words, and turn to the Lord: say unto him, Take away all iniquity, and receive us graciously: so will we render the calves of our lips" (14:1–2, AV).[1]

The cycle of the prophetic word is complete when God's people respond to God's word with their own articulations in life. That word comes through the prophets into the listening hearts of the people and there detonates like a bomb. The effect is the complete transformation of the inner life of the people, their return to God with their sacrifice. To formulate their own words—the stuff of their own living—is to bring forth the ultimate gift. For these words then express the deepest devotion of the people. The articulation itself places the finishing touches upon this process.

In this picture the prophet has great respect for the process of formulating one's own words. This can only happen at the end of the process when God's word shall have done its work, and shall have broken the hardness of man's own inner life, opening up his expressive abilities. God's word initiates; man's expression is in response. Moreover man's response in words is the fruit of his whole life. His liturgy is therefore ultimately his service. That is the cycle that completes God's work in His word.

Christians today do not need theological justification for seeking ways and means to express themselves in worship. In daily life they face the threat of mass depersonalization in a technological system. Computers do the work of many men. The particular gifts that always belonged to human beings have now been replaced by electronic and mechanical contraptions. The individual contributions of persons seem to be in little demand.

In a sensitive description of his experience in concentration camp, Bruno Bettelheim, in *The Informed Heart,* imagines our technological society to have many of the same pressures as were found in one of those camps.[2] A process of depersonalization is at work in society against which those who wish to survive with their personhood must struggle. They must find those personal disciplines which form their own life and identity.

Necessity of Expression

We have not as yet listened to his message. For we are in the stage of shouting out loud and long against the systems which oppress us. Everyone knows that he must express himself to retain his sanity. But the expressions at present are largely disordered shouts of pain and protests of freedom. They occur in "happenings" which suddenly break in upon our ordered ways.

Without these "happenings," however, our systematic routines would grind along as usual, completely bereft of our own expression. We even think of them as activities completely apart from us. The church's routines belong not to *us* but to *them.* We have objectified them as something over there. And with such division of areas of interest between that which expresses "our own thing" and that which is the expression of the system, there does not seem to be much hope beyond confrontation.

This is rather ridiculous for Christians. We have always insisted upon personal expression as absolutely necessary in worship. One must do his own living and dying. One's own faith must apprehend the grace of God in Jesus Christ and open up to God the Father. And the church has had its own traditions within which Christians can gradually open up to each other. Mutual encouragement on a purely human level has been a necessary part of the Christian life.

It is easy to forget this in congregational life because of our denominational existence. During these past centuries since the Reformation, the various Christian communions have developed their own specialized interests, and the total Christian program of growth has become fragmented. It is easy to let the enthusiastic groups take care of human expression in a denominational way while liturgical denominations "do their own thing." That was probably all right in a divided Christianity, but it developed specialized Christians who were then lacking in their general development. Today, with our emphasis on ecumenical growth, we must assume that congregations will themselves develop a much more variegated program: that expression and empathy will be the poles around which each congregation will worship.

This means that we must find those outlets where human expression can be nourished and developed to the place where it can serve as a vehicle for the worship of the whole congregation. Somewhere in the total program of the congregation we must provide for our "school of expression." And it cannot be expected that this will happen by itself. The ability to express oneself immediately is very rare indeed, and sometimes that is exactly what that person should *not* do. Instead, we need to develop teachers who can gently encourage persons whose expression has been injured at some time or another.

The case of nonsingers is a case in point. Ask a nonsinger who told him he couldn't sing, and you will discover that he will remember the time, place, and person who told him this. That traumatic experience damaged his nerve. It requires unusual effort by a trained person to undo the damage done.

The effect of our impersonal culture upon our own efforts at expression is just as dramatic in almost every area of human life. This requires, then, a concentration of programmed effort to open up human beings to their own humanity.

Available Help

Fortunately we have unusual help available to the congregation today.[3] A good deal of technical expertise has been engaged in opening up human lives. Sensitivity groups have swept the nation and have invaded our churches. At one time the aims of opening up human awareness almost overwhelmed congregations with techniques. This has been followed by a whole movement to uncover the unconscious world of sense perception; to awaken touch and smell; to heighten human awareness at the preconscious level. Those exploring the place of movement in language and action have rediscovered the dance as a total involvement of the body in language. Some churches have provided facilities for dance classes which unwind "uptight" members and open up a whole world of human movement.

The unrestrained explosions of the rock idiom immediately involve the young adherents in dynamic, compelling surges of rhythmic energy. The whole effect is so to engage attention as to completely release all inhibitions—"they blow their minds."[4] Such experiences, being of a more elemental type, do not really involve the person as an individual. They seem to belong to mass society, and the cooperative energies released in unison have some frightening characteristics. One cannot predict their end result.

More characteristic of genuine individual expression is the jazz idiom.[5] There individual musicians are carried away in improvisation which itself can be the communication of human experience. The individual players in a jazz group participate in very sensitive interhuman experiences as they cooperate in accompanying a fellow member as he "does his own thing."

There should be an organized place for presenting such expressions within the congregation. Occasionally the use of a public service for such expression is certainly in order, provided there is careful announcement of what is intended. A corporate liturgy is quite different in its aims and in its corporate demands from such a service of expression. That difference should be faced clearly.

A much better opportunity for the medium to be expressed in its own atmosphere would be separate services. One does not have to worry whether there will be a good attendance. There always is. This medium of expression can stand in its own right. It can be set up in a spectator-performer arrangement which will elicit the best from the performers, and allow the spectators to involve themselves as they feel called to do so.

Such opportunities then would allow the whole experience to mellow and to ripen into those forms which can best be introduced into the corporate worship as an expressive vehicle. We would have laboratories for the development of new types of materials that could constantly enrich our worship and give new life to old forms.

Pop-Art

A very careful line should be drawn between such contemporary techniques for expression and the faddish media that our people use. All of us whistle tunes that are currently popular and are heard on TV, radio, and in our daily world. Christians have always, more or less, used this material to express their own experience. Usually the experience, often very sentimental in its message, is on a very shallow level where most people can enter in.

Those of us who are older remember this pop-music as the so-called Gospel songs used in large revivals and evangelistic campaigns, or around a youth camp fire. We know how carefully we drew the line between the songs we sang in such settings, and the hymns we sang in church. In fact, many ministers have spent their entire lives in drawing just this line. Then, just when we had it pretty well set, the mood of the age changed.

Now pop-music is pretty well established among our youth not just as a popular commentary on the worship and life of the church but as that worship itself. Prayers are sung to the Gillette advertisement or to the tune of "Hernando's Hide-Away" with a flippancy which makes one wonder what the content of the prayer really is. The whole effort hides under the term of *contemporary* material. It would better be called pop-music.

One should not stop this development. It is always a companion to the more serious worship of the church, and it has a very important place in bringing people into more serious and deeper expressions. But there is a great danger today that this means to an end may become the end in itself. Certainly some materials will prove themselves in such expressive use. They can very well be introduced into worship at those places where expressive media are effective; or they can be used at services where all those attending naturally use such materials. The use of "We Shall Overcome," "Blowing in the Wind," "Where Have All the Flowers Gone," "Lord of the Dance" is pretty safe because of the testing they have had in other expressive places of life. On the other hand, until the whole congregation is given the chance to enter into this particular material as its own medium, it is too precipitous to throw it at them. One must remember that the young always try to do things differently; they don't actually expect adults to accept their standards. To impose this medium upon the whole congregation is quite imperialistic. In some ways it is to open the congregation to the tyranny of popular sales' techniques and promotion; for the interests of youth were never so manipulated as they are today.

On the other hand, some evidence of their expressive medium must be exhibited within the worship of the church if we expect young people to make the necessary effort to understand the media we use. Experience has shown that generally youth are extremely grateful for a little evidence of concern for their media, and they will be happy if a small open door is allowed them. They will use it to provide the rhythms and movements that the whole liturgy should always have.

Traditions of Christian Experience

There is traditional justification for the expression of Christian experience. Whenever the liturgies of the church became so formal that they failed to involve the expression of the people, some parallel institution arose for expression. And there was always friction between the two for a period of time until both were brought together in a new united revival of worship.

One remembers the rise of Pietism in the 1700s and the provision of pietistic meetingrooms in many of the German churches. There the members of the congregation could gather during the week for their prayer meetings and their songs. The Methodist movement centered in weekday meetings in the open and in homes where they could sing their own songs, most of which were set to melodies snatched from current secular tunes, accompanied with

126

a marked beat. And in our own day, the evangelistic tradition nourished by the Sunday school movement always lurked just a short distance away from the formal liturgy of the church, usually injecting its own media into those forms.

Thus there is nothing new or wrong with the use of present-day forms of the secular world to sing about one's faith. It has a long history. That history, however, has its own place parallel to the church's worship. It is our contention that this is where it should be. It should not take over that worship and substitute for the corporate liturgy of the church. Instead, its use should be developed through expressive media of its own, and a place for this whole expression should be carved out in the worship program of every parish. Then the materials which survive in this process can very well be used in the corporate liturgy. One can judge pretty well when the time has come for the use of such materials by their familiarity.

That the expression of experience will involve startling new forms must be taken for granted in our day. Those of us who are older were trained in routines which have completely disappeared from the scene. We do not realize the void that is left. We were trained in ordinary conversation over small things by long hours on a porch at night, rocking and talking with our parents and others. Today the porches are gone, the rocking chair has vanished as a talking-chair, and everyone has moved inside and fastened his attention on T.V. Party games were normal a generation ago. There we learned how to touch others, how to develop a sense of awareness of others. Though today we live closer together we have developed an isolated independence simply for self-protection. In other words, the much-heralded changes in human life in our time have also been quite destructive of human awareness. Though we can speak glowingly of our technological mastery over everything, we have in the process done a pretty good job of bottling up human expression.

Many of us are shocked to see how our young people try to rediscover their own humanity. "T-groups" and experiments in human awareness have grown up for their own sakes. The opening of human expression is no longer a means to an end, but has become an end in itself. It is then assumed that this end justifies any means at all. The results are always quite shocking to the "uptight" generation. The absence of restraining "manners" is only too evident.

The worst thing the shocked generation can do is to react in horror. We must appreciate the crying need for expression and provide those times and places in our congregational program where it can take place. Though we firmly believe that the highest forms of human expression come as responses to words/actions already filled with meaning by the acts of God, there is a clear relationship between one's own expression and his ability to open up from outside stimulation.

Perhaps the congregation of the future must have, on an elective basis, groups which are opening up individuals, expressing elementary Christian experience, learning to pray with their very own petitions, learning the rhythms and motions of dance, expressing themselves in the visual arts. Obviously it would be pretty awful to have them express their amateur selves in public worship weekly; but during the year, they could develop an offering that might very well enrich the whole worship life of the congregation.

Again we simply insist that though expression is absolutely necessary, times and places for such expression be found apart from the corporate services of the congregation. Our insistence is grounded on the nature of human expression. There is a discipline to expression that must be learned. Effective spontaneity is not simply the opening up of completely native gifts. It is the pouring forth of gifts that have been prepared for any moment's use—and this is something quite different. We need such expressive spontaneity in our worship desperately today. To find it, we cannot ignore those times and places where talent can be nourished and developed for that occasion.

Evangelistic Program

Though the word *evangelism* obviously derives from the Greek word for gospel or good news, we have used it for a variety of purposes. "Evangelistic meetings" are already identified in our minds with "evangelists" who preach in large meetings with song leaders, campaign oratory, and careful publicity. Actually, these evangelistic gatherings are really the prolongation of past forms of large outdoor rallies. Their purpose and their success is in warming over the embers of an old-fashioned faith. They are aimed at those who have heard the gospel, who respect the Bible, and who are brought back into a faith they once had.

It is really difficult to justify the use of *evangelism* for this activity. For to evangelize is really to proclaim the good news of what God has done in Christ for the world. One would think, then, that the world itself would be the locus of this proclamation —that is, some time and place where there is little reminder of the faith, some area of life within which all talk about the faith is inappropriate and embarrassing.

Such places are not just academic talk. They are realities within the territory of every congregation in our land. We have so organized our secular life as to compartmentalize every separate area. Within each compartment we follow certain accepted standards of action and speech. Inasmuch as our faith is usually reserved for the compartment of one day and one place, we have a host of compartments which are completely untouched by that faith.

Evangelism for a congregation should involve a careful survey of this compartmentalization of life in the neighborhood of the congregation and the actual selection of some place where the proclamation of the gospel will be attempted in *that* world. The process involves using the language of *that* world in *that* place to proclaim the gospel. This implies a much different program than most of us have imagined.

We have some models, however. For instance, during World War II in France, atheists, Roman Catholics and Protestants, and agnostics found themselves involved in the underground together. For the first time they were thrown together in a common, desperate task and they learned from one another. Directly after the war a group of Christian laymen gathered together to form the religious community at Taize, France. Concerned about the unity of the church and its service to man, they have used their experience in a new evangelism, centering in the concept of presence.[6]

They assume that most of the world has heard the message of the gospel, but it has been a message without accompanying deeds. Now the gospel must be spread by men and women who, in the fullness of their faith, dare to be present in the isolated compartments of man's life. Words are spoken when needed, but integrity of being in the midst of human life communicates best. With such a program these few individuals from this little community have influenced a whole world.

We merely select one model. Others are at hand. All insist upon the presence of men of faith in their integrity of being. Identification with other human beings on that deeper level which we are afforded by the gospel is the method of proclamation.

Through the last decade campus ministers have followed this model. They have had to. For the campus is usually quite isolated from the world of the church where the language of faith is natural. To minister among students one has to enter this world of religious estrangement. The so-called coffeehouse ministry was a most interesting experiment in evangelism. The students were provided with a meeting place in which they could feel natural and comfortable. In this setting one could fashion his own bridges into the world of faith. The lack of emphasis on the intuitive powers of man at that time gave the campus minister a chance to bring in poetry, visual arts, dance rhythms, etc., which with their broad dimensions of human experience, aided in the understanding of the gospel.

The coffeehouse was a pretty shaky bridge, though. Was it firmly set down within the natural world of the student or was it bogus and suspect? Did it really involve the student in the world of faith or did it just train an artistic avant-garde? These are questions that always lurk wherever men of faith enter the world of pure secularity.

One wonders whether when the church provides a coffeehouse it has really gotten into the secular world at all. Perhaps we should be present in places where coffeehouses already exist and *there* find ways of proclaiming the good news! And maybe that is not as hard as the halfway measures that we attempt because of our timidity.

This discussion has a direct relation to the worship of the church. We have a passion today for bringing the "world" into the church's worship. We rejoice that we have exposed the faithful to a jazz mass! But isn't a jazz mass really a pretty corrupt form? Should we try such halfway measures? Shouldn't we be present where jazz is performed and there learn to proclaim the gospel? If we did this, we would probably bring back some forms which were genuine in their human expression and not shaped for "religious" purposes.

It is our contention that evangelism should be a part of every congregation's program. Each congregation should determine some particular place in the world's life surrounding it where it should be engaged in the proclamation of the gospel. Then they should resolve to be present in their essential humanity, ever ready to speak of their faith when the occasion arises. We would assume that this is evangelism.

Such a program would remove the evangelistic emphasis from corporate worship where our people need the full nourishment of their faith and the celebration of the presence of God through Christ. Meetings of an evangelistic character in the old sense of the word should be part of the program for expression.

NOTES

1. The King James translation of "calves" is finessed by the RSV with "fruits" when the original Hebrew is "bulls." Eric Werner, the musicologist, has shown how the elders, at that time, after watching the priests in their rituals, then repaired to a side room in the temple and imitated their actions substituting their own words. This is what Hosea referred to. It is a very graphic mixing of words and actions.

2. Bruno Bettelheim's *The Informed Heart: Autonomy in a Mass Age* (New York: Free Press, 1960) has moved me deeply. I believe it says much more than was intended.

3. See John Killinger, *Leave It to the Spirit* (New York: Harper & Row, 1971). I believe this is an excellent summary of what is happening in the field of human awareness. I have not attempted to duplicate what he says. If I have been critical in my review (*Religion in Life*

[Winter 1971/72]) it is because I represent the opposite pole. When talking about expression, Killinger is excellent.

4. Benjamin De Mott says "that rock is a mixed experience, appealing at once to my sense of my sophistication and my sense of the unavailingness of my sophistication; that rock lifts me from the burden of knowing the good and yet believing my knowledge to be useless; that rock permits me to be part of others, not a mere resentful conscious self, not a perceiver harried on every side by multitudes of other conscious selves passing their 'distinct' values, opinions, interests, greeds forward into my space and notice; all these truths matter considerably. They establish that rock can possess quasi-religious force. It leads me past myself, beyond my separateness and difference into a world of continuous blinding sameness. For a bit it stoneth me out of my mind." *Supergrow* (New York: E. P. Dutton Co., 1969), pp. 57 and 58.

Should not the church raise a question about its use in worship?

5. Jazz is often a generalized term for any marked rhythm. I use it here in its more specific meaning as a most expressive medium within which the individual player is allowed a large space for improvisation within corporately established rhythms.

6. The concept of presence occupied the minds of Christian students the world over in the late fifties and early sixties. They picked it up from the experience of these groups. In its original meaning it assumed that the actual spacial presence of Christians in foreign areas of human life also brought into this space the disciplines surrounding the Lord's presence. To accomplish "presence" was true evangelism. In the cheapened form in which many seem to inherit such original concepts, the real context of presence has evaporated. One then thinks actively and rushes to "be where the action is." Of course "with what?" is the key question. Only in a solid recovery of *what it is* we do in worship will we open up the content of Christian presence.

11   Programmed
       Worship

We have urged congregations to make a thorough analysis of their total program of worship, dividing it into the various traditions of worship that are involved. Then successively we have considered these traditions: the Eucharist, the preaching of the word, family prayers, education into worship, Christian experience or expression, evangelism. We now come to the final tradition—that of programmed worship.

Some years ago as a member of the Commission on Worship and the Arts of the National Council of Churches, I attended a most confusing meeting called to consider the Christian calendar. It was hoped that representatives from the various denominations could make some progress toward a cooperative Christian year that all would celebrate together.

It was immediately evident that the group was sharply split into two different traditions. Those from so-called liturgical churches followed a fixed church year. It was divided into two roughly equal parts: the festival season from Advent through Pentecost when all followed the life of our Lord, choosing readings around the various events of his life; and the season of the Christian life in the power of the Spirit where lessons were chosen to bring one successively through the various parts of that life.

The majority of Protestants, however, while giving due place to Christmas and Easter and the seasons of Advent and Lent preceding these festivals, were wedded to a programmed approach to their calendar. That is, their attention was centered upon their people, their needs, the current events and holidays of the secular world within which their people lived. Such events as Rally Day, Men's Sunday, Women's Sunday, Youth Sunday, Race Relations Day, United Nations Day, Christian Education Sunday, Thanksgiving Sunday, Stewardship Sunday, were big celebrations which they hoped could be made general throughout the churches.

The "liturgical" churches were set into a pattern of fixed lessons from which there was little variation even for an earthquake. Preaching from these lessons became a separate art of opening oneself up to their message and then trying to elaborate on how the Spirit comes to us, through the lessons, in the middle of the particular mess we are in. That is an exercise in empathetic expression. The same round of lessons meets the preacher year after year. If he stays several decades in one parish, he will have worn a groove in familiar sections of Scripture. Though some churches have traditions of a three-year round of such lessons, and others are opening up this possibility,[1] the whole art of worship is in an approach to something which is quite objective, fixed, and not susceptible to immediate influence from the needs of congregational programs or current events.

On the other hand, the approach of other Protestants was frankly programmatic. Nothing was fixed. The order of service depended upon the church and the congregation in planning sessions. Inasmuch as the celebrations are all part of a programmed approach, the materials used are determined after the particular theme of worship is devised. They are threaded on the theme as beads are threaded on a necklace. The art is that of building up the effect upon the worshiper, of leading him into the theme, of leaving a clear message and duty with him, of moving him to action. Clearly wide possibilities lie before each planning session. Materials of all sorts can be supplied, discussed, and chosen. And a "worship service," therefore, is a creative act in which members of the congregation are involved.

Now it would be impossible to hold that these two positions are as drastically held to in the churches as our description would indicate. As we mentioned, many Protestant bodies have begun to celebrate seasons of the church year such as Advent and Lent. And the "liturgical churches" have been urged by their bureaucracies to program definite emphases for each season through "calendars of causes." Judging from the mail on the pastors' desks, this "calendar of causes" holds equal honor with the church year and intricate ways and means are found to program the causes into worship.

Perhaps the place where the two systems collide most often is in occasional services such as baptisms, marriages, and funerals. Here it is more or less assumed in our culture that those affected should have a part in the planning. In recent months it has become "the thing" for couples to plan their own services of marriage, and it is usually only a brave minister that will insist upon the stated liturgy of the church. The programmed method of constructing acts of worship seems to be in favor in an age of expression and relevancy.

The Case for Traditional Worship

We have taken the position that something essential to worship is lost if this approach prevails. For the approach is frankly man-centered. Worship is shaped to have an effect upon the thinking, feeling, and acting of the worshipers. All of the techniques of sales are then employed, along with psychological and sociological know-how. Worship becomes motivation for predetermined actions, and basically this is *not* worship of God.

Worship is the response of man the creature to God the Creator. As a response it is fixed upon the reality of God in his actions. The recital of those actions comes to us in a well-considered way of some kind. Perhaps the present church year and its lessons needs revision—it is certainly not holy in itself. It is created by men. But it is also the creation of the experience of many, many men; and we are in the process of improving it. It is the very best that we have got. And it does start with God's actions, encouraging their celebration. Some of us who have served two decades in the same congregation have found that the cycle of lessons intersects us constantly in different problems in life. There is a wholeness in what we are exposed to in these lessons and the liturgy which is far greater than the most inspired collage a talented pastor can bring together.

We would urge that the program of the congregation—its emphases for youth, men, women, race relations, etc.—be separated from the corporate act of worship. A great deal would be accomplished if this could happen. First it would clear up the intent of the use of language. Programmed worship is man-centered. The language is inflated to create its effect upon men, to get them to act. This is the language of advertising. There is nothing wrong with it. Men have to be motivated, and language must be used for this purpose. The consumer, however, will set up his defenses against it. He will accept only a portion of what the language claims for the product.

The language of worship, however, demands the use of words which are already filled with meaning by the acts of God and the experience of Christian people. This language invites the empathetic feeling of every worshiper. One must somehow relax the worshiper, insure him that he can open himself without being hooked, and expose himself at his own pace to ultimate reality. The language of the liturgy therefore leads in the opposite direction from that of congregational programs.

The Importance of Program

This is easy to say but the existence of the Christian church on this continent depends upon its program! Congregations are, in the Canadian and American scene, voluntary associations. They are made up of persons who, of their own free will, choose to belong, to contribute, and to share their lives. This forces the ministers as leaders of voluntary associations to live in an extremely political arena.[2] Reality demands that they face this openly. The political aspect of their leadership is openly seen in their management of the congregational program.

Moreover the only time when the congregation is gathered these days is at the main service on Sunday mornings. That is our problem: everything has to be thrown into that time and place. Announcements must be made. Areas of the program have to be promoted in some way. Program and worship have to come together.

Setting aside a short period of time for specific program announcements at worship is perfectly possible, provided the people learn to expect this to happen, and then have the opportunity to worship without program interruption. This can best be handled before the service starts (if enough have gathered), between some of the acts of worship, or just after the service. No matter what time is picked it will inevitably interrupt the feelings of some members at first. So rigidly have we tried to keep to forms and manners of worship that we have piled up introductory private acts of devotion before the service and after the service. These are certainly very helpful, and would be just fine if our churches were supported by taxes as in Europe. But we have simply continued this tradition without acknowledging the radical difference which exists in this country, namely, that our association is voluntary. The result has been that the minister has tried desperately to inject programmed material wherever he gets a chance. He must keep the association going and even more, direct it into meaningful channels. But he then becomes a promoter rather than a leader in worship and prayer.

Let every congregation face this dilemma squarely, determine how and where its program will be promoted and by whom. If this is to be when the congregation is gathered together, then let that be announced and expected. Then clean up your worship of God!

Occasional Services

The head-on clash between the contemporary and the traditional takes place in hidden areas. In those services which involve only several individuals such as marriages, baptisms, funerals, etc., the minister deals with persons who know little about the liturgies of the church. Sometimes they are very anxious for the official liturgy of the church in its most traditional form. One cannot explain how we have kept the words "plight thee my troth" in our wedding services to this day except that at weddings the majority want to enter into the tradition in its quaintest expression; just as the bride will wear her grandmother's dress.

More often, though, a couple will insist upon contemporary expression, having chosen passages from some poet, and having composed their very own promises. With the introduction of the folk idiom into liturgies, it is almost impossible to define the line between "sacred" and "secular" music. The argument is made now that there never was a difference between the two.

This is not the place for wishy-washy thought and action by the minister. Some years ago our Jewish friends, faced with the Christian confusion between the concepts of sacred and secular music, decided that in their tradition this distinction should not exist. After all, everything belongs to the world; the whole world belongs to God! They began by taking note of the central acts of the religious life where we take the things of the world and offer them to God, and then decided for themselves what they would take as "liturgical" music. They set certain standards for the use of music in the liturgy—standards formed from the demands of oral and corporate usage, memorability, etc. They gave these to their musicians. The result was a flowering of Jewish liturgical music. The composers had guide lines before them and they did not have to wander all over.

The experience is helpful for us. Actually we share this same background and can do the same thing. What is "secular" and what is "sacred" is obviously not determined by the unchanging nature of the piece; it has been determined, in the lack of specific actions, by associations. Wagner's Bridal March had sacred associations to our fathers, it has secular associations to us. Purcell's Trumpet Voluntary had secular associations to our fathers; it has sacred associations to some today.

In the absence of help from denominational commissions on worship, the congregation must make some decisions. The service of marriage does not belong to the bride and groom but to the church. On the other hand the marriage service of the church has followed the most traditional wishes of brides and grooms. It is difficult to describe the inherent integrity of the rite of marriage. The promises of bride and groom to each other in the presence of God and of witnesses is obviously the center of the act. These promises should of course be in terms that are understood by bride and groom, but they also must be in terms that express the Christian view of marriage in depth. It should be routine for ministers to go over the service of the church with every couple. Usually a full explanation is enough to welcome its use. But where this is not so the revision should be in keeping with its intent.

Where such an act is the center of the rite, we usually have accepted ways of framing this act. First there is a gathering together of the whole congregation so that they may enter into the meaning of the act. This can be accomplished by hymns and psalms and responsive readings. Then the Christian meaning of the act is conveyed through Scripture and/or an address. Following this the couple make their entrance into the act with their engagement promises, and then move to the altar for their marital promises. The pronouncement of the act and calling God's blessing upon it in prayer conclude the rite.

As with the services of the church, the action itself is the center of the rite, everything leading up to it or receding from it. To think of the rite in terms of this action is to see the problem of language in a different way. The problem of contemporary language is made much less all-inclusive. A few changes here and there, or a contemporary promise may be all that is needed.

Baptism

Congregations throughout the land are experimenting with new services of baptism. There is reason for this effort. Ecumenical discussions with the Eastern Orthodox and the Roman Catholics, together with our studies of biblical theology, have shown us that we have really doctored up the act of baptism in the centuries since the Reformation. The essential actions are no longer evident. Instead the emphasis is upon assurance that the belief of the sponsors is sufficient to support the Christian education of the baby in future years. The serious regard for the growing faith of the child is praiseworthy. However, ignored is the act itself, the presence and meaning of water, the threefold shape.

Hans-Ruedi Weber in his *Militant Ministry*[3] introduces his discussion of baptism with a memorable picture. Discovered on a mountain top on the island of Rhodes is a large rock, hollowed out, with steps on either side leading west and east. He imagines a baptism occurring on Easter morn at sunrise. The catechumens first stand at the west steps, face the darkness of the west and renounce the powers of darkness, knowing that they are taking a stand against political powers that could overwhelm them. They then are led into the waters and are pushed under three times, thus being identified with Christ in his suffering, death, and resurrection. They then ascend the eastern steps into the rising sun and the life of the Spirit. They are clothed with white robes and are given candles as symbols of this new life.

Here is the threefold shape of baptism, each caption separate and very clear. The shape of this threefold action is easily remembered. Luther insisted that the Christian enter into this memory every time he gets up in the morning and faces the world. His service of baptism keeps the actions clearly visible. It is merely since this time that we have lost them.

Experiments in services of baptism should follow this shape. We are still quite confused about where we should go as a church in a new service. The separation of confirmation from baptism in the Western church has taken the former act into a new context, but one which we cannot as yet define. In the other direction, there are a number of Protestants who would move far away from the actions and make baptism into a sentimental symbol.

In view of the uncertainties at this time in history, perhaps we should use the rite the church provides, but demonstrate the actions. Some congregations always have baptisms when the gathered congregation worships, substituting this act for a preparatory confession. A small table is placed in the aisle; water is brought and actually poured during the prayer (the sound of a lot of water splashing is something new!). Some symbol of the new life such as a baptismal garment is then placed on the baptized.

Funerals

The demand for a programmed approach to a service is present also at funerals. It is assumed that the character of the deceased will in some way shape what is done. The door is again open for the creative hand. We have always felt this pull ourselves. Yet there is probably no other place where the traditional liturgy of the church and the familiar readings are more effective. Everyone brings his own memories into the situation; the whole atmosphere is charged with the person. There is really no need to heighten this; in fact, there are great dangers in so doing. Instead, by concentrating on the service, whole passages jump out of their traditional setting and take hold which formerly were meaningless.

Every congregation should train a number of cantors in a service of the burial of the dead, making them familiar with sung responses and chants and hymns.[4] This training might take an evening. We have found these cantors very ready to take part whenever they are asked, and usually they count it a great privilege to be able to help.

The use of these trained cantors is possible wherever the funeral is held. A printed program will also involve the congregation. Involvement in the words of the liturgy at this time is probably more important than in other rites.

Again, the structure of the rite is simple. It consists of material which gathers the congregation into the action of prayer: litanies, psalms, hymn. Then we listen to Scripture, to readings, to an address. Prayers then follow—hopefully such prayers as will involve the people.

In considering programmed worship, we have set two approaches to worship against each other. We have then insisted that the congregation must separate its programmed materials from those it uses for the worship of God. A place must be found where the program of the congregation is pursued, but not in the midst of worship. In those areas of occasional services where the danger of programmed changes is greatest, we have insisted that congregations should start from the accepted rite of the church, opening it up to some personal expression. A little flexibility here will go a long way toward identifying the worshiper with that specific service. It will be "his own" service.

NOTES

1. Lutherans, Episcopalians, and Roman Catholics are working together in this effort today. The Episcopalians have just completed their three-year series, and are trying it out.

2. James Gustafson has written a very direct and perceptive article, "Political Images of the Ministry," *The Church, the University, and Social Policy,* Kenneth Underwood et al. (Middletown, Conn.: Wesleyan University Press, 1969), vol. 2. It urges ministers to bring this skeleton out of the closet and live honestly in its presence.

3. See the opening chapter in Hans-Ruedi Weber, *The Militant Ministry* (Philadelphia: Fortress Press, 1963).

4. I train a group in the chants, the Lord's Prayer in Anglican chant parts, and several hymns.

12 Education Into Worship

If the members of the congregation were polled as to their choice of materials for worship, that poll would reveal immediate preferences. Examination of these polls would reveal that the preferred materials bore no relation to their inherent value. Instead, one would discover that in every case the preferred material was taught to them in a careful manner.

All the great periods of hymnody were accompanied by an educational program. The Reformation chorale was taught by the village cantor, the Methodist hymn in the prayer meeting, the American hymn by Lowell Mason's schools in church music, the Victorian hymn in organized introductions of hymnals, the folksong revival through choir schools, Billy Sunday had his Rodeheaver, and every Sunday school its songleader. The hymn tunes were all taught to the people. Preference therefore develops from mastery; and mastery from a very careful process of training.

It is no wonder that today young people should prefer songs in their own idiom. One marvels at the time they put into learning to play the guitar, listening to others and imitating them, and then singing together. The results are neither particularly in the folk idiom or contemporary; they are just the idiom that is popular and that youth has presently found in favor. The popularity derives from a mastered familiarity.

This seems to be so obvious that it is difficult to see how we have so completely ignored education into worship in our churches. Despite the fact that we have developed a very intricate form of worship in most of our congregations, there is no comparable structure of education which would insure every worshiper of a process of mastery. Instead we merely assume that the forms will automatically catch hold of people in their use.

Several years ago a national commission on worship of a great denomination set up a conference on worship for leaders of the districts.[1] There was a search for congregations which had a full program of education into worship. The search at that time turned up three congregations throughout the nation, despite the fact that this denomination weekly used a highly sophisticated liturgy.

This opens up the heart of the problem of traditional worship. Art forms just do not automatically fit themselves as ready servants for each new generation. If they did we would need no system of public education at all. Yet we expect this miracle to happen in the church. The problem is not primarily with the tradition but with the absence of an educational program of any kind. True, some of the tradition is outdated and merely clutters up the service. But the majority of traditional material we use—when enthusiastically taught—can become the vehicle of the worship of our people, even today. It has been the assumption of this essay that renewal in Christian worship is best accomplished by such an educational program.

Dilemma—Education or Worship?

Practically every leader in the worship of the congregation feels the lack of congregational education. But it is pretty hard to provide the first steps toward this education. There is usually no lack of educative enthusiasm in the church school. Most of our church schools today are emphasizing the worship of the church as an essential part of their content. Unfortunately the people who attend the service of worship are not those who have received training. Public worship brings together a new congregation at every meeting and it is this specific congregation, gathered together on this particular morning, that has to use the forms with meaning.

An obvious answer is to intersperse educative directions throughout the service before each act the people make. At the time of the Reformation some of the reformers actually wrote liturgical directions in paragraphs preceding each action.[2] The actual worship was interrupted again and again by these wordy directions until the actions themselves were crowded out. This has been imitated recently by liturgical churches who have annotated masses, or sermons explaining what we do and why. Again, worship is turned into education, and we end up having something quite different from what we intended.

Because the educative process is rather difficult, some are ready to take shortcuts toward experimentation in worship. One such shortcut is to bring excitement into worship through specially trained performers. Choirs, musicians, dancers, can be brought in to do their own professional thing. This has always given the impression of novelty and freshness. But to the degree that it turns the actions of the people of God into a performance before spectators it fails in its objective. Except for very unusual congregations, our basic approach to worship must be congregational. We must involve every member in what we seek to do. We must find ways of doing this within the context of the congregational gathering.

Reassessment of Opportunity

The answer for many of us is in the reassessment of the various aids we have for congregational participation. The voluntary choir has been with us for a long time, struggling through its own special music and giving leadership to congregational singing. In many of our congregations this traditional choir has primarily focused on congregational leadership. Instead of weekly rehearsals of special numbers to be sung *at* the people, biweekly meetings are held for any and all who wish to learn the language of worship. Training is given in corporate conversation, responsive reading, singing hymn tunes with rhythm and movement, discovering new tunes. Those who attend rehearsals learn simple ways of intercommunication with each other when they are scattered in the congregation. Thus a fifth column of helpers is developed. Agreed gestures move from one to another in the midst of the congregational worship. The results are usually gratifying in the increased response of the people.

145

The training of at least a half dozen cantors in every congregation can be a great help. A cantor can take the load of leadership from the minister in a large part of the sung responses of the service. Then the use of two cantors, each introducing a chanted psalm for each side of the congregation antiphonally, springs loose a number of experiments. For instance, it is easy to chart a psalm on one note till the last word; then having the first side raise that last word one full note while the other side drops a minor third. The simple introduction of the first verse by the cantors gives all the information the congregation needs thereafter. Their use for the first line of hymns often eliminates the need for an accompanying instrument. A few such trained persons who know a standard number of congregational responses can give a whole congregation the confidence it needs in response.

Often ministers concerned about education into worship will have a prelude of short instruction. This will occur after the organ prelude. It is admittedly a practice session but if it is done naturally and reverently, it can be a very proper introduction to worship. The line between education and worship can be sharply drawn by the concluding remark, "Now let us worship our God." And the service begins. It would be a little much to do this every Sunday, but frequent use of prelude time can do a lot for congregational participation. Instruction immediately before the use of material is eagerly followed by the congregation; they remember it vividly long enough to experience the difference it makes. It carries over for several weeks. Furthermore, it establishes a mood for worship within which mistakes are forgiven, and playful effort is encouraged. Very few persons will oppose new material if they are given opportunity to learn how to use it just before use. In fact, reactions are almost always positive.

Every opportunity should be taken to help the people into the new ways. Rhythm makers, movements, directions that they can see somewhere are not at all out of place. Members of the congregation should know who is in charge of tempos and rhythms and some effort should be expended in making this easily visible. Occasionally a hymn or a response quickly heads for disaster. Usually a congregation is so tense that everyone is conscious of impending failure but no one dares to do anything about it. It flops and everyone looks the other way. We should be loose enough in our worship to stop when things are going poorly, admit what is wrong, and try again. God is not mocked by such creaturely admissions of failure; he may be pleased with the second effort.

Essential Disciplines

When a service of worship demands congregational responses, it has already assumed the existence of some practice and skill. Corporate response as one voice is certainly a discipline that implies prior practice. It does not just happen. Yet one rarely finds a congregation where the skill has been carefully developed. We usually just assume that everyone knows how to adjust his voice in a speech chorus, adopt the proper volume, and thus form the common voice.

Learning this discipline is probably the first step in education into worship. The teacher starts with a safe assumption that present errors will be evident. Most of us read silently for our own information. When we read out loud, we do it at the speed of this silent reading, and in a conversational, sing-songy voice. If these voices are put together into long responses the results are most unedifying. The tones of the phrases are always alike, and inevitably give off the sound of boredom. Leave responsive reading to the natural efforts of the congregation and the service will quickly go to sleep.

One has to practice how to project one's voice into a corporate sound. The whole voice of the congregation should sound as one, but usually in a very quiet sound. Noisiness in speaking is usually the sign of those who are used to lead. They should remember that—even for the leader—a congregation is made up of all voices blending in one voice.

It cannot be assumed that hymn tunes are easy for everyone to sing. In our American churches we have collected the tunes of many different traditions and eras of church history. Each tune belongs to its own family and has its own characteristic tempo and rhythm.[3] This is not immediately obvious. However, the inquisitive worshiper can easily make his self-study of these tunes by consulting his index, setting up his own categories by dates and source, and then studying the brothers and sisters in one family together.

Organists, in "giving-out" the tune should indicate the tempo that will be used without any change. A sloppy habit of slowing up the tune just before the people start is a sure way to invite insecurity. In some churches with chorale traditions, where all tunes are sung approximately the same way anyhow, the old tradition of chorale preludes may actually introduce a chorale or provide interludes within the singing. Whereas this is a fine variation for relieving boredom and can bring in talent to dress up a tune, steady use of this technique ignores the tremendous variety of tunes we have in our hymnals on this continent, and the need for a clear statement of intention by the organ to introduce a tune.

Simple canon forms like "When Jesus Wept" by Billings have been used by congregations through simple announcements in the printed program: "Sung as a round: All once through; Right Front, Left Front, Right Back, Left Back will sing successively." Usually it is safe to send pretrained members of the choir, or cantors, into each section—perhaps putting some mark of identification on them. A single monument of confidence can establish the tone of a section.

Within every order of worship there should be some place where one can always find new material. Many churches find responses to read lessons the traditional—and helpful—place for such material. Some churches have made up little mimeographed booklets for each season which are placed in the pew racks. These songs are used as responses to lessons, and also during the administration of the Holy Communion. In each case they are sung very quietly. This is the place for accompaniment by recorders, woodwinds, strings, or guitar. The accompanying instrument then gives the tone to the piece. A typical list of such songs in one of our congregations is as follows:[4]

For Lent and Easter:

> When Jesus Wept; Wondrous Love; Gethsemane; Amazing Grace; Love Is Come Again; Lord of the Dance; Canticle of the

Sun; Praise the Lord Who Reigns Above; Our Risen Lord; Brother On Me; O For a Thousand Tongues; Hilariter.

For Christmas and Advent:

Lovely Child, Holy Child; Sussex Carol; Creator of the Stars of Night; The King Shall Come When Morning Dawns; On This Day Earth Shall Ring; We Praise, O Christ, Your Holy Name; The Quempas Carol; Unto Us a Boy Is Born; I Wonder As I Wander; My Lord, What a Morning; The King of Glory.

For Pentecost Season:

The Devil Wore a Crucifix; All Who Love and Serve in the City; What Will I Do?; The Truth From Above; Simple Gifts; My Dancing Day; Lord, Bring The Day To Pass; Through All the World Below; Here at Thy Table, Lord; The Call.

Where this is tried there is almost complete enthusiasm for the practice. In addition, a good number of new pieces become familiar, chosen from a wide background.

Other congregations have replaced the choir use of the Psalms —the introits and graduals—with the congregational use of the Gelineau Psalms. At present there are enough of these psalms available in print to procure and use. The melodies are quickly caught by ordinary people. The rhythms are easily managed by children's rhythm choirs. Such openings for new material bring a freshness into our stagnant worship and bring it alive.

The Use of Lectors

It is encouraging to see congregations make use of laymen in the reading of the passages from Scripture. Too long has the worship been dominated by one ordained leader. The practice of using laity restores the meaning of the whole event—the Scriptures come alive in the midst of a believing congregation.

Unfortunately we assume that every layman is automatically able to read meaningfully, to project his voice so that it can be heard, and to provide the silence necessary for comprehension by his hearers. Actually, these are rare gifts in a day when we don't generally read aloud. One just cannot assign responsibility for reading by a calendar and assume that the results will be edifying.

We should reserve the function of lector to those who will acquire the skill. They must be available for practice. The practice session will be aimed at slow reading, the general musical quality of the sentence rhythms with variety of tone, the avoidance of the prevailing habit of allowing the last words of a sentence to drop in pitch into oblivion. Because public reading requires projection of one's voice, it is quite different from conversation. The reader has to speak to the person at the back of the church. This need for projection is what causes professional ministers to develop an almost chanted type of speaking—the "pulpit-tone." At least they can be heard!

Once a group of lectors—men and women—have been trained, there are duties they can perform. There is a loud cry from the young for secular readings which can accompany those from the Scripture. It is assumed by them that the Holy Spirit did not die with the early church, and that perhaps men and women since then have had something to say; and perhaps it might be more relevant. The lectors can be the group that collects and screens such readings for use as comments on the appointed texts, or as preparatory material for worship.

Training in Prayer

Congregations should also have a group in training for leadership in prayer. The very thought of training in the leadership of corporate prayer does violence to our popular image of the prayer leader. We have assumed that free prayers just pour out of certain gifted individuals, and that they have a direct pipeline to the Holy Spirit.

A little investigation will show that everyone who prays has been trained to pray. Where no training is provided the gift of free prayer dries up. A wise older pastor who had the marvelous gift of free expression in prayer once told me that he always fastened his mind upon some texts from the Psalm, which he knew by heart. He would then start with these and allow them to pull him into his own expression over against them. Present studies of the folk preachers show that they always start with some fixed intention. The response of the congregation and the whole setting then pulls them into the midst of journeys they would never have imagined themselves.

A number of techniques can be used by a few trained laymen to unwind members of the congregation and provide them opportunity to express their own petitions. At the final service of the Uppsala Assembly of the World Council of Churches, a procession of young people entered the center aisle with posters and placards, each representing some world cause for which we should pray. The young people then spread all over the cathedral among the worshipers, pushing their placards before the eyes of the congregation in each place and thus soliciting prayer. This was a dramatization of what can be done by concerned persons. It would be good to have banners made which would draw forth our petitions, and have them brought up with the offering, and then displayed one by one, requesting the people's prayers.

Some liturgical churches have experimented with various forms of petitions which will be offered by the presiding minister or deacon repeatedly until members of the congregation have discerned the style. Then petitions in this form or thanksgivings are solicited from those present. Litanies are readily used when a trained person can just inform the congregation what its particular. response will be. Each change will bring forth a short direction.

Processionals

We have lost the sense of a processional as an act of worship for the congregation. Most congregations reserve the procession for getting the choir to their seats and then one has to be gowned to join in. The procession of the people has completely disappeared in our day of fastened down pews and precise manners. Yet we have kept materials such as the Kyrie within our service even when their processional character is gone. Of course the next step would be to eliminate the Kyrie altogether as some rites are doing.

151

But there is another direction of movement—toward reestablishing the processional of the people on special occasions, and then reinvesting such processional material with the original meaning. In the Western rite the Kyrie is such material. It is a litany sung as an act of entrance into the presence. The simple litany form, "Lord, have mercy" is the response the people make in procession to their places. Some churches have started their services with an act of entrance, providing the Kyrie in its extended Eastern form ("In peace let us pray to the Lord. LORD HAVE MERCY.") as an actual people's procession. The procession goes around the church several times and those members who want to join in the walking do. Easier, perhaps, is the use of a processional hymn. Whoever wants to celebrate the day with a joyful hymn comes out of his place in the congregation and joins the choir and ministers in procession or recession.

It is hard to realize how completely our people are fastened down to the floor with the pews in our worship. Such processions bring about a marvelous change in attitude. Young children jump at the chance to move. Rhythms are easily discovered. Here is where the dance almost comes into worship—and it is the dance of the congregation, not of specialists.

While we have listed some specific helps into education for worship, we have merely sketched the outline of the effort. More extended treatment is presented in several other books: *Liturgy and Life* and *O Sing Unto the Lord*.[5] We have insisted that the primary problem of our current worship is really not its irrelevance to our day, or its ignorance of the contemporary scene. It is lifeless because no life is being constantly poured into it through education.

An institution is in its death throes when its rites and ceremonies are highly structured and yet the worshipers do not know what they are doing. If there is not a vibrant program of education and change apparent to all, those who have come into the ceremonies lately—the young—find no foothold where they can join in. To restore our institution to its lively and meaningful stage, we must open it up to a constant flow of new materials. We must provide in its regular structures those well-planned opportunities for everyone to join in what is going on. Education into worship is essential and long overdue.

NOTES

1. I was part of the search in the United Lutheran Church in America. It was in the early sixties, I believe. I doubt if the situation has changed.

2. See particularly the liturgies of the great Swedish reformer, Olavus Petri. They were works of art in his hands: they fell to lower depths in the hands of others.

3. I have provided help for such practice in my *O Sing Unto the Lord* (Philadelphia: Fortress Press, 1966).

4. In University Lutheran Church, Cambridge, Mass.

5. See Henry E. Horn, *Liturgy and Life* (Philadelphia: Lutheran Church Press, 1966), and *O Sing Unto the Lord.*

Epilogue

We started our study of Christian worship with a frank acknowledgement of the collapse of landmarks. This collapse has been accompanied by the sprouting forth of short-lived experiments and "happenings" while the faithful cower in fear of the future and in defense of what they know.

We attempted to come between these two poles with a reorientation of imagination, of our social view of reality, and of our language that might be adequate for the present as we now know it. Within this reorientation we then took a second look at the traditions that now make up Christian worship, hopefully with an aim toward renewal.

The new and innovative is so much with us as to demand little attention in this volume. Other guides exist for the use of new material. We have simply insisted that, whatever the materials, a sufficient program of education be devised for the introduction of materials to all the people. A successful liturgy is that which most easily does what it is supposed to do: involves the whole people in conscious acts in God's presence—acts which they understand and freely offer.

In the absence of landmarks, we have urged a new beginning of setting our own standards to define and regulate Christian worship within our modern context. We have insisted that, if this were done according to the nature of the Christian experience and the demands of corporate actions, a movement of renewal would blossom in our churches.

Theologians often speak of God's actions in history, of God's word. We know that God's actions and word are set within the human context. Worship is a large part of that context within which great things happen. Therefore our understanding of worship is as important as anything we attempt in the Christian life. It is to this end that we have offered this book.